Fifty Hikes in Vermont

Ascending Camel's Hump

Fifty Hikes in Vermont

Walks, Hikes, and Overnights
in the Green Mountain State

The Green Mountain Club

Fourth Edition

A Fifty Hikes™ Guide

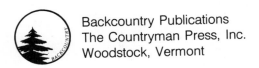

Backcountry Publications
The Countryman Press, Inc.
Woodstock, Vermont

An Invitation to the Reader

Over time trails can be rerouted and signs and landmarks altered. If you find that changes have occurred on the routes described in this book, please let us know so that corrections may be made in future editions. The author and publisher also welcome other comments and suggestions. Address all correspondence to:

Editor
Fifty Hikes™ Series
Backcountry Publications
P.O. Box 175
Woodstock, Vermont 05091

Library of Congress Cataloging-in Publication Data

Fifty hikes in Vermont: walks, hikes, and overnights in the Green
    Mountain State. — 4th ed. / Green Mountain Club.
        p.   cm. — (Fifty hikes series)
    "A Fifty hikes guide."
    Rev. ed. of: Fifty hikes in Vermont / Heather and Hugh Sadlier.
    1985
    ISBN 0-88150-167-0:
    1. Hiking — Vermont — Guide-books.   2. Backpacking — Vermont — Guide
-books.   3. Vermont — Description and travel — 1981- — Guide-books.
I. Sadlier, Heather.   Fifty hikes in Vermont.   II. Green Mountain
Club.   III. Title: 50 hikes in Vermont.   IV. Series.
GV199.42.V4S22   1990
917.43'0443 — dc20
                                                                89-18634
                                                                CIP

Published by Backcountry Publications
A division of The Countryman Press, Inc.
Woodstock, Vermont 05091

Printed in the United States of America
Typesetting by Sant Bani Press
Series design by Wladislaw Finne
Trail overlays by Richard Pusey, Charthouse

Cover photograph and interior photographs by Bob Lindemann

Foreword

Publication of this fourth edition of *Fifty Hikes in Vermont* begins a new phase of the Green Mountain Club's relationship with Backcountry Publications. In a sense, this project began several years ago, when Backcountry approached the GMC about updating the hikes in an earlier edition. Conditions in the field change constantly, so GMC staff and volunteers field-checked and rewrote many of the existing hike descriptions. When the time came for a new edition, the next logical step was for us to start fresh and prepare a completely new version of the book.

The Green Mountain Club is a volunteer organization, and this project is an excellent example of what volunteers can accomplish. *Fifty Hikes in Vermont* was written for the Green Mountain Club by Mary Deaett and Bob Lindemann, two people who epitomize the dedication of GMC members. Bob has spent much of the last two summers hiking the trails of Vermont, drafting trail descriptions and maps, and taking and developing photographs. Mary has spent her time at the computer and on the phone, researching background information and drafting the manuscript. Thanks to their dedication to the Green Mountain Club and this project, *Fifty Hikes in Vermont* will provide enjoyment to the hikers of Vermont as they explore the natural and scenic highlights of the state.

Brian T. Fitzgerald, President
Green Mountain Club

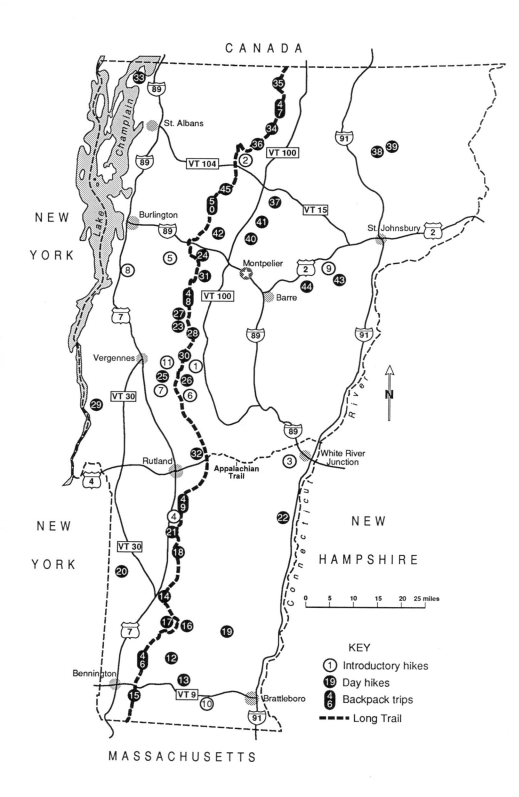

Contents

Central Vermont 87

Northern Vermont 119

Weekend Backpacking Hikes 161

Acknowledgments

As with any book, there are always a host of people who provide invaluable assistance. Any Vermont hiking book would be difficult to write without the Green Mountain Club staff, especially Katherine Borchert, executive assistant, who went "beyond the call of duty" in office support; Ray Auger, field supervisor, who reviewed all fifty hikes and provided detailed information on the southern hikes; and Sue Lester, field assistant, who gave similar details for the northern section.

We would also like to thank the following people: Ben Davis, Smith Edwards, Jan Edwards, and Brian Fitzgerald for reviewing the hikes; Mark Haughwout for checking southern hikes and providing most of the fire tower information; Joseph Cook and Earl and Edna Williams for checking southern hikes; Chris Wood for checking trailhead information and reviewing the text; the United States Forest Service, especially Fred Putnam, Middlebury District; the Vermont Department of Forests, Parks and Recreation, especially Diana Frederick, Barre District, and Laura Hollowell; Sharon O'Loughlin, geologist/information specialist, Agency of Natural Resources, for sending information on Mount Philo; John Wrazen, director of the Babcock Nature Preserve at Johnson State College; Don Whitney for sending information on the Ascutney Trails Association and Crystal Cascade; David Bailey, director of the Green Mountain Audubon Nature Center; and Reidun Nuquist for writing the history of the Green Mountains.

We would also like to acknowledge that much of the historical and geological information in this book was derived from State of Vermont, Agency of Natural Resources brochures and other publications. We are indebted to their research and cooperation in providing information to us.

Mary Deaett
Bob Lindemann
for the Green Mountain Club

Introduction

You are about to explore one of Vermont's greatest treasures—the Green Mountains. They offer hours and days of hiking enjoyment in late spring, summer, and fall.

This book guides you through the mountains along a variety of Vermont's hiking trails, from easy walks to ambitious day hikes to weekend backpacking trips. All these hikes offer you crisp mountain air and beautiful wilderness scenery, most with breathtaking views of surrounding pastoral valleys and neighboring mountain ranges. You can hike along sparkling streams, over suspension bridges, across open summits, and through ferned, secluded gulches. Choose the hikes that excite and appeal to you the most.

While we encourage your enthusiastic exploration of Vermont's hiking trails, we also caution you to consider your health and conditioning, your experience in the woods, the weather, your equipment, and a variety of other factors before exploring Vermont's backcountry wilderness. Please read the advice and information in the following section carefully before beginning your journey. Be prepared and be informed, and then thoroughly enjoy a safe journey into the Green Mountains of Vermont.

How to Use This Guide

The approximate distance and hiking time, vertical rise, difficulty rating, and the map that illustrates the area are listed at the beginning of each hike. This information is designed to help you select a hike which is within the limits of your hiking ability and the time available for your outing.

Total distance is the total number of miles you will hike on the trails described. Each hike description indicates clearly whether this distance refers to a loop, a return by the same route, or a one-way hike (with cars spotted at both ends of the trail).

Hiking time includes all time spent walking or climbing and some time for resting and enjoying the views. Allow extra time for meals and swimming or fishing in the streams and ponds en route. Times given are for a leisurely but steady pace and allow for differences in terrain. If you follow any alternate or side trails not included in the total distance, remember to adjust your hiking time accordingly.

Vertical rise is the total amount of climbing along the route. It may occur all in one climb, in which case it is the difference between the lowest and highest points on the route. But it may and frequently does occur over several climbs. If there are descents between these climbs, then the vertical rise noted for the hike will exceed the difference between the lowest and highest points on the hike. Substantial vertical rise can turn even a short hike into a real challenge.

Difficulty ratings are easy, moderate, and strenuous—with a few hikes falling in-between. *Easy* hikes are accessible to most people, including first-time hikers, and are especially good for families with children. *Moderate* hikes require a de-

Bridge on Mount Pisgah hike

gree of stamina; some previous hiking experience is advisable. *Strenuous* hikes are challenging outings for experienced hikers in good physical condition.

Maps are listed at the beginning of each hike so that you can obtain supplements to the maps printed in this guide. The maps that appear in this book are based on United States Geological Survey (USGS) or Green Mountain National Forest (GMNF) topographic sheets.

Although the USGS maps are sometimes out-of-date, they may be helpful to you. They can be obtained from some sporting goods shops and bookstores, or they can be ordered from the USGS by writing to: USGS Map Distribution Branch, Box 25286, Denver Federal Center, Denver, CO 80225 (303–236–7477). You can also order USGS quads from two other sources. The National Survey, Topographic Office, Chester, VT 05143 (802–875–2121) stocks Vermont and New Hampshire quadrangles. Timely Discount Topos has access to USGS quads for all states. Timely Discount will take your order by phone (800–821–7609) and then ship your order the day after they receive your check or money order. All maps purchased through Timely Discount are on a prepaid basis only, but orders are fulfilled very quickly.

GMNF maps may be ordered from the Forest Supervisor's Headquarters, Green Mountain National Forest, P.O. Box 519, Rutland, VT 05701 (802–773–0300 or 733–0324 V/TDD). GMNF maps only include those quadrangles in which the forest is located. You must also send a prepaid order to the supervisor's office in order to receive these maps.

The maps in this book are intended only as general guides to the trails. Because of logging, development, and other wilderness disturbances, trail locations sometimes change, though every care is taken to ensure that trail descriptions and maps are accurate at the time of publication.

This book begins with several introductory hikes, which we recommend for new hikers or for those who haven't hiked recently. The introductory hikes are also appropriate when your hiking time may be limited but you still want to enjoy Vermont's beautiful scenery. The book ends with a selection of weekend backpacking trips.

The other hikes are organized geographically to offer you a variety of hiking terrains and different scenery representing each region of the state.

Before you begin your hike, carefully plan your route, equipment, and supplies. Be sure to allow adequate time for unpredictable weather changes, and remember to leave a copy of your itinerary with a friend.

Hiking Season

The ideal time to hike in the Green Mountains is the summer and early fall. Most of the trails are not blazed for winter use and are, therefore, frequently impossible to follow.

Vermonters joke that spring never comes to Vermont—winter leads directly into "mud season"! When warmth does come to the valleys, trails in higher elevations become wet and muddy. Hiking during "mud season"—from mid-April to late May—can cause a great deal of damage to trails. Please wait until the trails are completely dry before hiking.

The average monthly temperature in June, July, and August is in the 60s, in September the high 50s, in October the 40s, and in early November the mid-30s. However, the temperature can drop below freezing at any time of the year!

Insects can be a problem throughout the late spring and summer. "Black fly season" usually lasts from mid-May until mid-June, but black flies can be a problem throughout the summer in certain locations. Mosquitoes are also a nuisance at dusk and dawn, especially in wet or swampy areas.

Safety

Vermont weather is extremely unpredictable, with the possibility of high elevation snowstorms even in the summer! Rain and fog are common, and storms can be sudden and dangerous. If there is any threat of stormy weather, either do not hike at all or select a hike at a lower elevation, and be sure to bring adequate rain gear, a wool sweater, and a hat. Even on short hikes, always bring along a compass (learn how to use it first!), a first aid kit, and a supply of prepared, high energy foods like nuts and dried fruits.

Water can be polluted even in the most pristine mountain environments by an intestinal parasite called *Giardia lamblia*. Giardia is very unpleasant, often resulting in severe dysentery and vomiting. Treat, boil, or filter all water before using, or for the majority of hikes in this book, simply carry water with you.

Unfortunately, vandalism of cars at trailheads is a problem; remove all valuables from your car, or at least lock them in your trunk.

Again, remember to leave your itinerary with a friend, stay on your planned route, and sign in at all registers. In case of a missing hiker, vandalism, or any other emergency, please contact the Vermont State Police.

Most of the trails in this book are blazed with either white or blue paint.

Important turns and intersections are indicated by arrows or double blazes (one blaze over the other). You should always be able to see the next blaze ahead of you. If you do not see a blaze after a few minutes, stop, look, and backtrack to make sure you are still on the trail.

Clothing and Equipment

The most important rule for clothing, even in summer, is to dress in layers or bring extra clothing with you. The shirt that feels cool with perspiration on a hot summer day, may chill you to the bone on the summit of a mountain where it is windy and cold. You should always take along an extra layer for protection.

Boots — Because most of the trails in this book are primitive footpaths, not specially surfaced trails, you will need to wear a good pair of boots that provide adequate support and traction. Two layers of socks — the first cotton, the second of medium weight wool — are recommended.

Poncho or rainsuit — Remember, Vermont weather is unpredictable, always be prepared!

Wool sweater or jacket — For comfort and protection against winds and cooler temperatures at higher elevations.

Wool hat — 40% of body heat is lost through your head.

Day pack
Guide book, maps, and compass
Water bottle or canteen
First aid kit (moleskin or similar product for blisters, bandaids in assorted sizes, triangular bandage or bandana, adhesive tape, anticeptic cream, gauze)
Trail lunch (and extra food for emergencies)
Flashlight with working and extra batteries
Matches
Pocket knife

Insect repellent
Sunglasses (optional)
Camera and binoculars (optional)

Additional items required for backpacking trips:
Frame pack
Tent
Sleeping bag and pad
Stove and spare fuel
Cooking gear
Extra clothing
Garbage bags (pack out *all* trash!)

Trail Courtesy

Private Property—Many of the trails in this guide are located on private property. Please be considerate and appreciative of these landowners and treat their property with respect to ensure that trails on private property remain open. Please do not block traffic or access to private homes when parking at trailheads, and always be sure to check with landowners before parking on private property.

View from Elmore Mountain

Pets—Although your pet may be your best friend, please leave your pet at home. It is often difficult to prevent pets from contaminating water supplies, and pets frequently have problems with wildlife, especially porcupines. If you still choose to bring a dog with you, please be sure to keep it leashed.

Trash and Waste—The Green Mountain Club has one firm trail motto: "Pack It In, Pack It Out." No litter should be left on the trail or in the woods. Because human waste can damage water quality, use outhouses when available, or otherwise bury human waste six inches deep at least 100 feet from any trail or water supply.

Camping and Fires

Camping and fires are restricted on most Vermont lands, depending on whether the land is private, state, or federal. Please contact the Green Mountain National Forest, Vermont Department of Forests, Parks and Recreation, or the Green Mountain Club for more information.

Peregrine Falcons

The following trails in this book pass by the nesting sites of peregrine falcons: White Rocks (hike 4), Mount Horrid Overlook (hike 6), Mount Pisgah (hike 38), and Elephant's Head (hike 45). Because the falcons are very sensitive to human disturbance, especially from above, some of the trails are closed during their nesting season.

Peregrine falcons have finally returned to Vermont after a thirty-year absence. These beautiful birds were almost eliminated by the use of the pesticide DDT after World War II. After DDT was banned in 1972, the Peregrine Fund at Cornell University and the United States Fish and Wildlife Service started a re-introduction program. Captive-born young falcons were released on many cliff sites throughout the east. The peregrine release, or "hacking," program in Vermont is sponsored by the Vermont Institute of Natural Science, the Vermont Department of Fish and Wildlife, and the United States Forest Service. The first wild nesting pair returned to Vermont at Mount Pisgah in 1985.

Bringing these magnificent birds back to Vermont is extremely important. Please obey any posted signs and do not disturb the birds.

The Green Mountains

The Green Mountains were part of an extensive inland sea until approximately 350,000,000 years ago, when pressure and heat transformed this region into a high mountain range. The mountains were then shaped and formed, until just 12,000 years ago, by thousand-foot-thick Ice Age glaciers.

The average elevation of today's Green Mountain ridgeline is 2,000 feet, although five peaks exceed 4,000 feet: Mount Mansfield (4,393), Killington Peak (4,241), Mount Ellen (4,083), Camel's Hump (4,083), and Mount Abraham (4,006).

Below 2,400 feet, you will find a mixture of northern hardwoods, like sugar maple and beech. A transitional forest, which occurs between 2,400 and 3,000 feet, includes yellow and white birch, and red spruce. Above 3,000 feet balsam fir dominates, along with some remaining red spruce.

The Green Mountains have long played an important part in the lives of

Vermonters. In addition to being an abundant source of clean, fresh water, they are vital as a timber and recreational resource. While significant numbers of white people did not settle in Vermont until the end of the French and Indian War (1763), archeological finds document the presence of Native Americans as far back as the Paleoindian period, or about 8,500 B.C. Abenakis lived and foraged here, as well as Iroquois. The richest sites have been excavated in the Champlain Valley in northwest Vermont, along the rivers draining into Lake Champlain, and in the Connecticut River Valley. State archeologists constantly add to our knowledge of Native American history.

White settlers were of predominantly Anglo-Saxon stock and came north from Connecticut and Massachusetts for cheap and plentiful land. They settled where the land was most fertile; like the Abenakis, they chose the Champlain lowlands and the Connecticut River Valley. They also cleared land along Vermont's first two roads, Crown Point Military Road and Bayley-Hazen Military Road, both of which traversed the Green Mountains. In 1791, the first Vermont census reported 85,000 people living here.

The population boom, however, was short-lived. The rocky state was largely unsuited for farming, and when the Erie Canal opened in 1825, westward migration began. People became a major export, along with potash, wool, lumber, dairy products, granite, and marble. Today the only signs of abandoned farms are the cellar holes and stone walls encountered by hikers on the lower slopes of the Green Mountains.

The mountains, once an obstacle to east-west travel, have become an economic asset. Within easy driving distance of major population centers on the eastern seaboard, they are visited by thousands of skiers, hikers, hunters, snowmobilers, and bicyclists every year. Tourism is now a major industry in Vermont.

The Green Mountain Club

Since its founding in 1910, the Green Mountain Club's primary purpose has been to build, maintain, and protect hiking trails and shelters for the enjoyment of Vermont's residents and visitors.

In 1910, the GMC founded the Long Trail (LT), the nation's oldest long-distance hiking trail. In addition to the 265-mile LT, which follows the ridgeline of the Green Mountains from Massachusetts to Canada, the Long Trail system also encompasses over 175 miles of side trails and sixty-three rustic cabins and lean-tos. This entire system is managed and maintained by Green Mountain Club seasonal field personnel, permanent staff, and hundreds of dedicated volunteers, in cooperation with private landowners and state and federal agencies.

In 1985, the GMC learned that thirty-four of the sixty-five miles of the Long Trail on private land in northern Vermont were for sale. Rising real estate values, the unsettled economics of the forest products industry, and rapid development in Vermont have created a volatile land market. The GMC also faced serious problems with landowners who wanted the Long Trail removed from their property or who wanted to use the land for purposes incompatible with the trail.

The Green Mountain Club was convinced that the scenic quality, environment, wildlife habitat, and continuity of the Long Trail must be saved. Consequently, the Long Trail Protection Campaign was started and important results have been achieved. As of July 1991, over $1,850,000 has been raised toward the $2.5 million goal, and approximately 26 miles of the Long Trail have been permanently protected.

The effort to save the Long Trail must continue. Vermont is experiencing a construction and population boom, and tremendous pressures on land use. Over 33 miles of the Long Trail are still in need of protection. The Green Mountain Club will continue the effort to preserve these high mountain lands that are so important to Vermonters and the thousands of people who visit the state each year.

Membership in the Green Mountain Club is the best way for you to support the protection and preservation of the Long Trail system, and the GMC is open to anyone interested in hiking and in Vermont's mountains.

If you would like to be involved in local outdoor and trail activities, you may join one of the GMC's Sections (chapters). Each section schedules hikes, other outings and social events, and is responsible for maintaining a specific portion of the Long Trail. You may also choose to become an At-Large member, if you are interested in supporting the Green Mountain Club, but not interested in joining a section. Benefits are the same for both types of membership: a subscription to the GMC's quarterly newsletter, *The Long Trail News*; discounts on hiking maps, guide books, and other publications; and reduced fees at most GMC overnight camping sites or shelters.

If you would like more information on the Green Mountain Club, the trails in this book, or other hiking opportunities in Vermont, please contact us. We'll be happy to help you plan your next hiking adventure.

The Green Mountain Club, Inc.
P.O. Box 889
Montpelier, VT 05601-0889
(802) 223-3463

Hiking information available from the Green Mountain Club:

The Green Mountain Club issues a variety of publications about hiking and backpacking in Vermont and welcomes inquiries about trail conditions and planning. To order the GMC publications listed below, see the order form in the back of this book.

Guide Books:
Guide Book of the Long Trail — (23rd Edition 1987, Fifth Printing 1991); pocket-sized guide with 16 color topographical maps. Complete description of the Long Trail, its side trails, and shelters; hiking suggestions and helpful hints.

Day Hiker's Guide to Vermont — (3rd Edition 1987, Third Printing 1990); companion volume to the *Guide Book of the Long Trail*. Comprehensive coverage of more than 200 short hikes throughout the state; 12 color topographical maps and 34 black-and-white maps; hiking tips and suggestions.

Trail Maps:
End to End, Topographic Maps of Vermont's Long Trail — (1988); set of 21 topographic maps that cover the entire Long Trail. The maps use four-color USGS quads for a base, and add Long Trail information in red.

Camel's Hump — (1985); color, fold-out topographical map of the Camel's Hump area; weather resistant, with trail mile-

Trillium along Stowe Pinnacle hike

ages, overnight facilities, trailheads, regulations, and other information.

Mt. Mansfield—(1989); color, fold-out topographical map of the Mt. Mansfield area; weather resistant, with trail mileages, overnight facilities, trailheads, regulations, and other information.

Mt. Mansfield Booklet:
Tundra Trail—A Self-Guiding Walk: Life, Man and the Ecosystem on Top of Mt. Mansfield, Vermont—This 12-page booklet with illustrations describes a natural history hike along the Long Trail on the summit ridgeline of Mt. Mansfield.

Green Mountain Club History:
Green Mountain Adventure, Vermont's Long Trail—(1st edition 1985, Second Printing 1989); an illustrated history of the Green Mountain Club by Jane & Will Curtis and Frank Lieberman. Ninety-six pages of rare black-and-white photographs and anecdotes of the GMC's first 75 years.

Pamphlets:
Day Hiker's Vermont Sampler—Folder with map of Vermont and descriptions of several hikes throughout the state; hiking tips and suggestions. Free with legal size self-addressed stamped envelope (SASE).

The Long Trail: A Footpath in the Wilderness—Folder with information and suggestions on hiking the Long Trail. Free with legal size SASE.

Winter Trail Use in the Green Mountains—Folder containing basic information about using the Long Trail system in winter. Free with legal size SASE.

Patches and Decals:
Long Trail Patch and Decal—Decal and fully embroidered patch in three colors—golden yellow and two shades of green. 3½" x 4⅛".

GMC Patch and Decal—Two-color patch with twill background embroidered in yellow and green. Decal in green and white. Both 3" round.

Other Resources

For additional information on hiking in Vermont, you may wish to contact one or more of the following organizations:

On federal lands:
Forest Supervisor
Green Mountain National Forest
P.O. Box 519
Rutland, VT 05701
(802) 773-0300, (802) 733-0324 V/TDD

On state lands:
Department of Forests, Parks, and Recreation
Agency of Natural Resources
103 S. Main Street
Waterbury, VT 05676
(802) 244-8711

On the Appalachian Trail (*AT Guide to New Hampshire and Vermont*):
Appalachian Trail Conference
P.O. Box 807
Harpers Ferry, WV 25425
(304) 535-6331

Key to Map Symbols

- - - - main trail

• • • • side trail

⍋ Appalachian Trail

Ⓧ campground

⇄ lookout

Ⓟ parking

𝚷 shelter

∿ brook

∘∘∘∘ stone wall

—•—• dirt road

⊐⊏ gate

Texas Falls

1

Texas Falls

Total distance: 1.2 mile loop
Hiking time: 1 hour
Vertical rise: 160 feet
Rating: Easy
Map: USGS 7.5' Bread Loaf

Impressive waterfalls and geological formations make this interpretive trail an enjoyable, easy hike through part of the Green Mountain National Forest. Texas Brook is part of a watershed that drains this nine-square-mile area. Beginning approximately three miles to the north as a seasonal stream, the brook makes its way to Hancock Branch, the White River, the Connecticut River, and finally into the Atlantic Ocean.

To reach the trail, drive west on VT 125 from the VT 100/VT 125 intersection in Hancock (0.0) to the signpost for "GMNF Texas Falls Recreation Area" at 3.0 miles. Go north on the access road to a small parking area on the left at 3.5 miles. (Additional parking is available at a picnic area up the road at 3.75 miles.)

The trail begins opposite the parking area where you see and hear Texas Falls. Elaborate stone steps and walls descend to the falls and provide breathtaking views into the deep ravine.

Cross the bridge over Texas Brook, turn left, and ascend upstream on more steps. You soon reach a registration box, which provides interpretive pamphlets for two interconnecting nature trails. The first trail follows the stream for 0.3 mile, then takes the road back to the

parking area. The second trail continues along an upper trail 0.75 mile in a loop back to the falls. Benches along the way allow you to linger, read the guide, and enjoy the trail.

As you walk upstream, still in sight of the brook and road, note the exposed roots and rocks along the trail. This erosion is caused by people walking off the trail and compacting the ground so the roots are unable to penetrate the hard soil. Please help stop further erosion by staying on the trail.

As you continue your hike through the evergreen forest, be sure to enjoy the fragrant air. The pamphlet explains that evergreens are "ever green" because their leaves are more efficient than those of deciduous trees at retaining life sustaining water during the winter. Adaptations include a smaller surface area, a waxy coating, and an antifreeze-like resin.

As you gently climb along the wide, gravel trail, be sure to look for an old aspen tree and lichens that appear on boulders. Also, take time to rest on one of several benches. The trail continues along a fern-covered bank to the crest of a hill. Hike down the hill, look for a bridge, and read the plywood disk de-

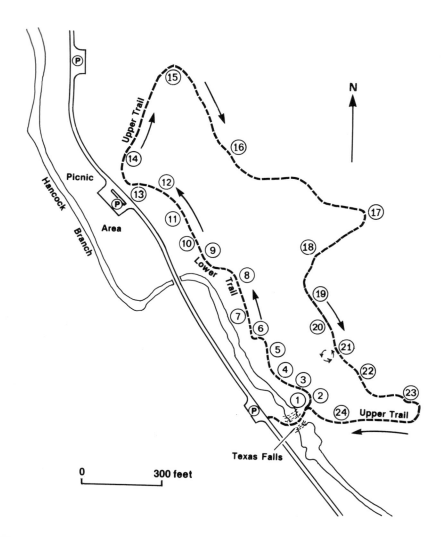

signed to help you identify area trees. At 0.3 mile drop off your pamphlet at the registration box and descend to the road and your car, or continue along the upper trail.

To continue your hike, turn right and climb along an old logging road that is also used for winter snowmobiling. The trail soon takes a sharp right and climbs to the top of the next rise, as you pass through a stand of mixed hard and soft-wood trees. At 0.6 mile, you cross two small brooks and then descend to a hemlock stand. Continue downhill to the falls and over a bridge. After a few steps and switchbacks, follow the loop trail down into the gorge. A side trail to the left descends to a lookout. At 1.1 miles, return the pamphlet to the registration box, recross the brook, marvel again at the beautiful falls, and continue to the picnic area for lunch.

2

Prospect Rock (Johnson)

Total distance: 2 miles
Hiking time: 1.5 hours
Vertical rise: 540 feet
Rating: Easy
Map: USGS 7.5' Johnson

This short hike offers superb views, including Whiteface Mountain and the Lamoille River as it meanders through the valley below and empties into Lake Champlain.

From Johnson (0.0), drive west on VT 15 to the Lamoille River bridge at 1.5 miles. Just before the bridge, turn right (north) on the Hogback Road and continue to a five car parking area at 2.2 miles on the left at the top of the hill.

Before or after your hike be sure to take the short walk through the woods by the parking area to view the Lamoille River and Ithiel Falls, a set of Class 2–4

rapids where the river narrows between two cliffs.

From the parking area follow the paved road northwest 0.1 mile to the Ithiel Falls Camp meeting grounds. Ithiel Falls Camp is a religious family camp with a series of cabins and buildings. Turn right and follow the white-blazed Long Trail up the gravel road opposite the cabins and past a rock outcrop. Halfway up the bank a small sign indicates an incorrect trail length of six tenths of a mile to Prospect Rock. Remnants of old cabins from the camp are seen along the short gravel road. Please

View of Prospect Rock (Johnson)

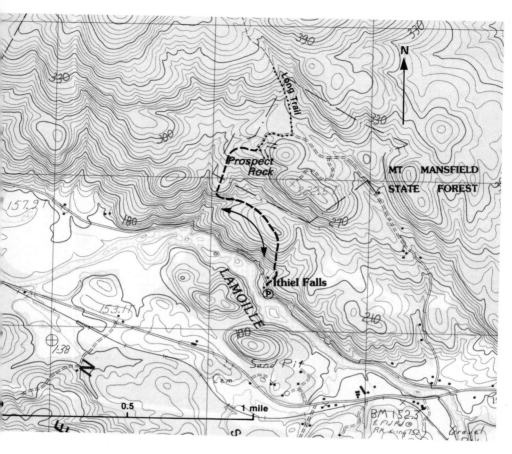

remember that you are on private property and should respect all lands and buildings.

The trail soon turns left off the gravel road and enters the woods where a new sign indicates a correct distance of 0.8 mile to the Prospect Rock overlook. Cross a small brook and ascend to another brook. Now following an old logging road, the trail zigzags up the hill. At 0.4 mile you cross a wet area on puncheon, a small wooden bridge of one or more log or board planks held off the ground on sills, and return to the old road.

Large boulders line the trail as you hike on almost level ground through a forest of mixed hard and softwoods. Climb along steep switchbacks, then ascend more gently until you see the end of the Prospect Rock outcrop and enter an area filled with ferns and raspberry bushes.

At 0.8 mile the trail makes a sharp right, ascends the steep hillside, then levels off and opens up onto Prospect Rock. Avoid the numerous spur trails as you head onto the rocks. After enjoying the spectacular views of White Face Mountain, Daniel's Notch, and the Lamoille River Valley below, hike back down the trail to your car.

Quechee Gorge

Total distance: 1.5 miles
Hiking time: 45 minutes
Vertical rise: 250 feet
Rating: Easy
Map: USGS 7.5' Quechee

This easy hike features spectacular views of the 155 foot deep Quechee Gorge and the Ottauquechee River. The name Ottauquechee comes from the Natick Native American word meaning "swift mountain stream" or "cattails or rushes near a swift current."

Quechee Gorge was formed approximately 13,000 years ago, toward the end of the last glacial age. Around 19,000 years ago, when the climate warmed significantly, the most recent glacier began to recede. A natural dam of debris (rocks, gravel, sand) formed in Connecticut and created a narrow lake, Lake Hitchcock, up the Connecticut River Valley. Similar lakes developed along the Connecticut River, including one in the Ottauquechee Valley. When the dam in Connecticut broke and Lake Hitchcock drained, water trapped in the Ottauquechee Valley also broke through its dam and drained. The gushing water quickly carved through the sand and gravel to the bedrock below. The river's tremendous force and natural scouring abilities continued to carve deeply into the bedrock. At the bridge, you can see the glacial sand deposits and underlying bedrock.

This figure eight–shaped hike can be reached via Exit 1 off I-89. If you are driving south on I-89, drive 2.5 miles west on US 4 from the exit. If you are driving north on I-89, drive 3.2 miles west on US 4 from the exit. (The exit ramps are 0.7 mile apart on US 4.) Just before the bridge on US 4 over Quechee Gorge, turn right on Dewey's Mill Road, opposite the Vermont Information Center. Continue 0.1 mile to the "Overlook Picnic & Parking" area. The trail is located at the back of the picnic area.

From the picnic area, turn right and hike 0.2 mile to a dam, hydro-generating station, and Dewey's Mill Pond. The dam was the location of the old Dewey Woolen Mill, but is now a lovely waterfall. Retrace your steps back to the picnic area, and follow the gorge trail of crushed stone and bark behind the gift shop and under the US 4 bridge.

The gorge was once a popular resort and the river provided power, but they were very difficult to cross. Early bridges often collapsed or were swept away by the current. The original bridge spanning the gorge was a railway bridge built in 1875 for the Woodstock Railroad. Historian William Tucker

Quechee Gorge

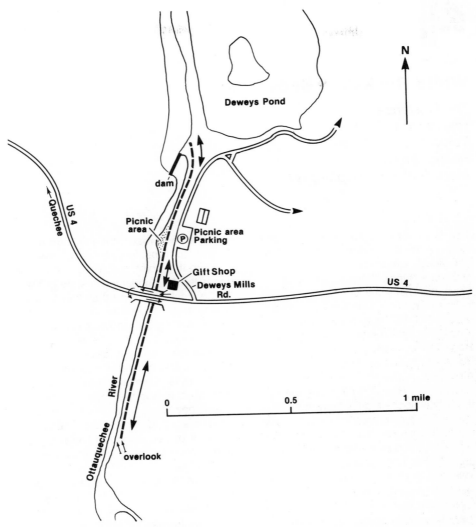

Deweys Pond

N

dam

Quechee

US 4

Picnic
area

Picnic area
Parking

Gift Shop
Deweys Mills
Rd.

US 4

River

Quechee

Ottauquechee

0   0.5   1 mile

overlook

claimed that "nearly 3,000 people assembled to celebrate the long antici-
pated event." The present steel arch
was built for the railroad in 1911, but in
1933 the tracks were removed and replaced with US 4.

Continue your hike along the chain
link fence, which protects you from falling into the gorge as you descend the
gorge wall to an overlook. Enjoy the
views deep into the gorge. Explore the
overlook area, and return to the US 4
bridge at 1.5 miles.

After going under the bridge, a trail
by the gift shop leads onto the bridge
where a pedestrian walkway is provided
on both sides of the road. Loop the
bridge for additional views into the
gorge, then return to the parking lot and
picnic area.

White Rocks/Ice Beds Trail

Total distance: 2 miles
Hiking time: 1.5 hrs
Vertical rise: 460 feet
Rating: Easy
Map: GMNF Wallingford NW

This relatively easy hike offers wonderful views of the White Rocks Cliff and the "Ice Beds," where ice, formed beneath the rocks during the previous winter, flows in a meltwater stream.

To reach this interesting trail, drive east on VT 140 from the VT 140/US 7 junction in Wallingford (0.0) to Sugarhill Road at 2.2 miles. Turn right, drive about 150 yards on Sugarhill Road, and turn right on United States Forest Service (USFS) Road-FR 52. Continue to the White Rocks Picnic Area at 2.8 miles. The picnic area has ample parking for thirty cars, along with picnic facilities and outhouses. (Note: The picnic area is also the trailhead for a different trail—the Keewaydin Trail—leading 0.8 mile to the Long Trail.)

Near the entrance to the picnic area there is a trailhead sign for the blue-blazed Ice Beds Trail. You immediately pass through a small wet area on bridges and turnpiking, a raised trailbed formed by placing logs on either side of the trail and filling between them with dirt and gravel. Large rock outcrops appear on the left and boulders dot the area, as you hike up the hillside. The trail swings to the right and climbs through boulders and softwoods. Hike

along a switchback, then ascend more steeply to a trail junction at 0.3 mile.

From this point, the White Rocks Trail leads left to a spectacular view of the White Rocks Cliff and the Otter Creek Valley to the southwest. A talc mine in South Wallingford on US 7 is also visible.

Because peregrine falcons have returned to this area and may be nesting on the cliffs, the White Rocks Trail may be closed during their nesting season. These beautiful endangered birds are easily disturbed from above. Please obey all posted signs, and refer to the introduction for more information about the falcons.

Return to the junction and continue uphill along the Ice Beds Trail. Enjoy the good view back to White Rocks before you hike behind the ridge and have only limited views to the north. The trail is quite rocky in this section, so watch your step. The trail soon levels before descending towards, then away from, the base of White Rocks Cliff. At the double blaze, turn right and begin a rocky descent. Follow the blazes along a series of small switchbacks, as the trail becomes less steep and more wooded. You begin to hear a brook to the left,

White Rocks Mountain from Ice Beds hike

White Rocks and Ice Beds **31**

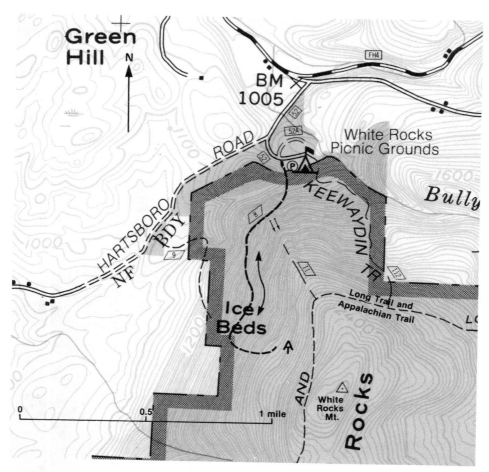

and the air feels cool and damp.

After descending a few steps, you reach a junction with an old road where you go left and downhill. Cross a brook on a small bridge and follow along the valley floor. You soon cross the brook again, ascend slightly, and at 1.0 mile reach the Ice Beds, where the brook you have been following emerges from the base of the White Rocks Slide.

The USFS sign at the location reads, "A shattering of cheshire quartzite rock probably occurred during the ice age to create this rock slide. During the winter,

ice and snow accumulate in the depths of the rock crevices. A continual down-draft of cold air in the shaded canyon helps preserve the ice and snow during the summer. The stream flowing from the rocks is fed by the melting ice. This keeps the water temperature at approx-imately 40 degrees throughout the summer."

After enjoying this cool, refreshing re-treat (especially on a hot summer day!), hike back via the same trail to the picnic area.

Hires and Sensory Trails
Green Mountain Audubon Nature Center

Total distance: 1.25 miles (for the two hikes described)
Hiking time: 1.5 hours
Vertical rise: 200 feet
Rating: Easy
Maps: USGS 7.5' Hinesburg, Huntington

Both of these easy trails are located in the Green Mountain Audubon Center, a 230 acre nature center owned and operated by the Green Mountain Audubon Society, a local chapter of the National Audubon Society. The grounds are open every day from dawn to dusk. The Visitor's Center is open weekdays and weekend afternoons, depending on staff availability. The center offers a Summer Ecology Day Camp, seasonal programs, workshops, classes, and more. We recommend that you pick up their brochure and map of the trails at the Visitor's Center. Donations to maintain the center are welcome, and you can also purchase a variety of books and other items. Please remember to stay on the trails and do not remove any natural objects from the area.

The Hires Trail goes to a lookout with an unusual view of both Mount Mansfield and Camel's Hump. The Sensory Trail, with a rope leading through fields and woods, is designed as both a hiking trail for the blind and visually impaired, and as a way for others to enjoy and experience the area through their other senses.

To reach the Green Mountain Audubon Center, take Exit 11 off I-89 (0.0) and turn left (east) on US 2. Drive 1.6 miles to Richmond and, at the traffic light, turn right (south) on Bridge Street toward Huntington. At 1.9 miles you cross the Winooski River. The road bears right and winds uphill before leveling again. Stay on the main road, as it bears left at two junctions. At 6.7 miles you reach a sign and turn right to find the center. Parking for eight to ten cars is located at the Visitor's Center, where there is a trail signboard showing the location of the numerous hiking trails.

HIRES TRAIL: This trail was named for Christine L. Hires, the woman who donated the land for the center. The trail starts to the right, behind the signboard. Hike up a short bank, bear right at an obscure junction, and climb some old wooden steps through young, mixed hardwoods. You quickly reach a junction with the Fern Trail on the left. Stay on the Hires Trail. Notice that you are hiking parallel to the Sherman Hollow Road, as you walk up the hillside on moderate grades. You soon bear left and climb through birches and then small softwoods. A bench provides an excuse to take a rest break and enjoy the tranquility and wildlife.

Continue uphill to a spur trail on the right which leads to Lichen Rock, a large moss-covered boulder. Return to the main trail and quickly reach a junction. Follow the unblazed main trail uphill along several rock outcrops, until you pass through mixed hardwoods and reach a rock shelf called "Lookout Rock" at 0.4 mile. Enjoy the nice views of Camel's Hump and an unusual view of Mount Mansfield to the left. From the overlook, gradually descend through young, mostly maple, hardwoods, until you are below the overlook. You soon intersect the other end of the Fern Trail and begin a moderate descent to a junction with the Sensory Trail on the right. Leave the woods, enter an overgrown field, cross a mowed lawn, and reach the Visitor's Center at 0.7 mile.

SENSORY TRAIL: This very unique

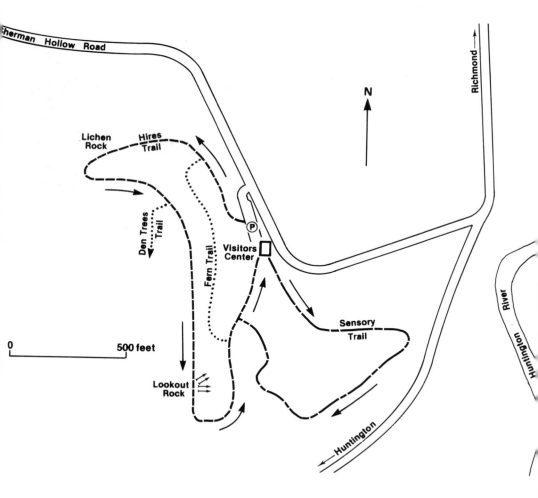

Camel's Hump from Green Mountain Audubon trail

trail begins on the porch of the Visitor's Center, crosses fields, winds through the woods, and at 0.5 mile loops back. What makes the trail unique is its design for the blind and visually impaired. A rope, strung between posts, provides a guide for the trail. For those who are not blind or visually impaired, close your eyes and notice the difference without the security and benefit of sight. You begin to rely more strongly on your other senses, and more fully appreciate the sounds and smells around you. Any description would be woefully inadequate—this trail must be experienced to be enjoyed!

Mount Horrid Overlook

Total distance: 1.25 miles
Hiking time: 1 hour
Vertical rise: 620 feet
Rating: Moderate
Map: USGS 7.5' Mount Carmel

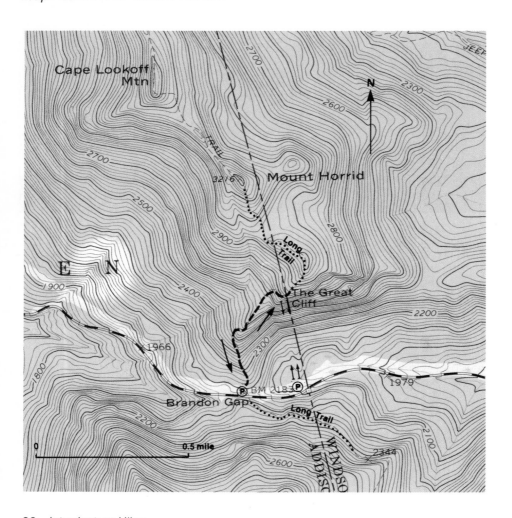

This short steep hike takes you to the top of the "Great Cliff." According to a Green Mountain National Forest sign, "the rock that makes up the exposed face of this cliff was formed during earliest geological times. Freezing and thawing have wedged off fragments which have accumulated over time on the mountain slope."

Be aware that the trail may be closed when peregrine falcons are nesting on the cliff overlook. Falcons last nested on these cliffs fifty years ago, though a nesting falcon pair, released several years ago, has returned to the area. Peregrine falcons are extremely sensitive to human disturbance, especially from above, and may abandon their nest if approached too closely. Please obey all posted trail signs during nesting season, and see the introduction for more information on the falcons.

To reach the trail, take VT 73 to the top of Brandon Gap. Just west of the gap summit, there is a new parking lot for thirty cars on the south side of the road. Before parking your car, however, stop at the pull-off area just east of the gap summit for a view of the cliffs and a beaver pond, as well as information boards describing the cliffs and pond ecology.

After enjoying the views, return to the parking lot and park your car. Cross VT 73, climb the bank, and begin hiking north on the white-blazed Long Trail. You cross a small raspberry patch and ascend to a Green Mountain National Forest register box and sign that indicates a distance of six tenths of a mile to the "Great Cliff" overlook.

After the sign, the trail steeply ascends on log steps to a ridge at 0.2 mile. Birches line the trail along the ridge, until you ascend more steps. The trail swings to the western side of the ridge, passes through mixed hardwoods, and becomes much rockier and steeper. Climbing steeply over rock steps that may be slippery if conditions are wet, you must watch your step and stay on the trail to limit erosion in this area. After hiking through some rocks, notice a birch stand just ahead and an opening in the trail at 0.6 mile. As you step out into the opening, you are on top of the 2,800-foot Mount Horrid Overlook seen from the parking area now 700 feet below you. Also below you is the beaver pond you saw from the pull-off.

After enjoying these views and of Bloodroot Gap to the south, hike back down the same trail to Brandon Gap at 1.25 miles. The descent is easier, but watch your footing, especially on steep sections in wet conditions.

7

Falls of Lana

Total distance: 1.1 miles
Hiking time: 1 hour
Vertical rise: 240 feet
Rating: Easy/Moderate
Map: GMNF East Middlebury

Falls of Lana

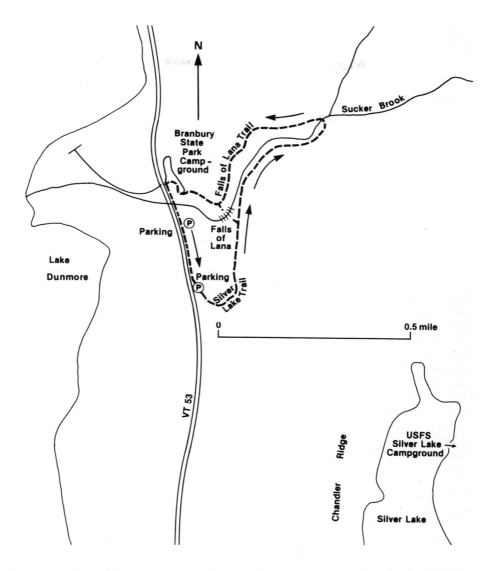

The Falls of Lana were discovered in 1850 and named by a party of soldiers for their commander, General Wool. During a tour of duty in Mexico, General Wool was known as General Lana, the Spanish name for wool.

The trail begins on Green Mountain National Forest land, leads behind the falls to a picnic area (be sure to bring lunch!), and descends to the Falls of Lana. The trail then follows a Branbury State Park trail into the state park campground and ends with a short road walk back to your car.

The trail is located on VT 53, 6 miles north of VT 73 in Forest Dale or 3.5 mile south of US 7 near Middlebury. A United States Forest Service (USFS) sign marks the correct parking area 0.2 mile south of the Branbury State Park entrance on the east side of the road. Be sure to avoid the first USFS "Falls of Lana" parking area 0.1 mile south of the park!

Although somewhat obscure, the trail climbs the small bank behind the parking area and quickly reaches the gated USFS access road to Silver Lake. Turn right and follow the road on easy grades. You soon reach a signpost that indicates you are entering the Green Mountain National Forest Silver Lake Recreation Area, and that motorized vehicles are prohibited to "preserve the quiet so seldom found in today's world." It also indicates a distance of one half mile to the Falls of Lana, and one and a half miles to Silver Lake.

Ascend the road along switchbacks, until you enter a clearing where a powerline and penstock descend from Silver Lake to VT 53 below. The penstock is a pipe that carries water from Silver Lake to a power station on the road. Through the clearing are views down to Lake Dunmore. Beyond the powerline cut, the road begins a gradual ascent and soon reaches a wooden sign on the left, as you start to hear Sucker Brook and the Falls of Lana. Behind the sign you can look down to the falls.

The road now parallels Sucker Brook and at 0.5 mile reaches the Silver Lake Trail junction and some outhouses. Continue parallel to the brook until you cross it on a wooden bridge about 100 yards from the trail junction. Just beyond the wooden bridge, you reach another blue-blazed trail junction which leads straight ahead to Rattlesnake Cliffs.

At this junction turn left on the Branbury Park Trail and enter the Falls of Lana picnic area, complete with a water pump, located just above the falls. Although there are very few blue blazes, walk through the picnic area and look for a rocky point at the west end. The trail swings to the right of this point, enters the woods, and reaches a junction on the right with another Branbury Park trail. Follow the main trail around the rocky point, until you enter a "rock valley" and reach an overlook with views of Lake Dunmore, Mount Independence, the Adirondack Mountains, and the Lake Champlain valley.

From the overlook, rapidly descend the rocky trail. Red blazes in this area mark the park boundary. Look for a pool in Sucker Brook below you, and just before the pool, turn left onto a rock overlook to see the Falls of Lana. After enjoying the beautiful falls, follow the trail as it swings right and away from the falls into a rocky, quiet, coniferous forest. Be careful to watch for blazes, as the trail descends to a plateau, makes a sharp left, and continues to the campground. As you enter the campground near the outhouse, walk straight and then bear left at 0.9 mile back onto VT 53. Turn left on the highway and back to your car at 1.1 miles.

Mount Philo

Total distance: 0.2 mile (plus optional 1 mile summit road walk)
Hiking time: 1 hour
Vertical Rise: 50 feet
Rating: Easy
Map: USGS 7.5' Mount Philo

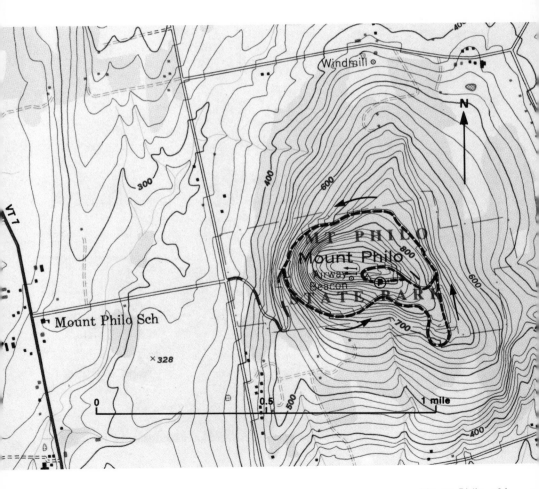

View from Mount Philo

This very short, easy trail provides an excellent view of New York's Adirondack Mountains, a nice opportunity for a picnic lunch, and the option of a one mile road walk around the summit area. The trail is located in the 160 acre Mount Philo State Park.

To reach the trail, drive 1.2 miles north on US 7 from North Ferrisburg, or 2.5 miles south on US 7 from the flashing light on US 7 near Charlotte. Turn east at the blinking yellow light to Mount Philo State Park (0.0). You reach the park gate at 0.5 mile. A day use fee is charged.

Drive through the gate and ascend Mount Philo by car. The road soon forks and becomes one way. Notice remnants of old roads and paths, concrete steps, an old spring, culverts, and a gravel pit. The summit cliff is on your left, as you drive to the southwestern side of the mountain for the final pitch to the top of the toll road.

At the top, you reach a contact station, a parking lot for fifty to sixty cars, and a large picnic area. The station and a firetower were established in the mid-1920s. Between 1938 and 1940 the Civilian Conservation Corps (CCC) constructed a steel tower which was abandoned by the 1960s and finally removed in the early 1970s. The CCC was a government work program during the Great Depression of the 1930s.

Your mini-hike starts at the western end of the parking lot, where you descend past a picnic pavilion to a large rock face with guard rails.

As you stand on the summit of Mount Philo and overlook what is now the Champlain Valley, contemplate that Mount Philo was once an island in the Champlain Sea. According to a booklet published by the State of Vermont, two different areas of rock were thrust over each other approximately 4.7 billion years ago: This low-angle thrusting was succeeded by high angle faulting. The Park rocks were subjected to weathering and erosion for over 300 million years or until glaciers advanced over the area less than 60,000 to 70,000 years ago. Advancing glaciers scoured the rock; retreating or wasting glacial ice left deposits of clay, sand and gravel in the Park. A series of lakes formed south of the northward wasting glacial ice and deposits of beach-gravel and lake-sand formed along the slopes of Mount Philo, which was then an island. An arm of the sea next advanced southward into the Champlain Valley leaving marine beach-gravels just west of Mount Philo. The marine waters retreated and present-day Lake Champlain came into existence.

Just north of the rock overlook, a trail descends to an even better vista. Return to the first overlook and, if you choose, hike the summit road loop, which provides additional views to the west and south.

Owl's Head
Groton State Forest

Total distance: 0.5 mile
Hiking time: 30 minutes
Vertical Rise: 160 feet
Rating: Easy
Map: USGS 15' Plainfield

This relatively short hike takes you to the summit of Owl's Head in Groton State Forest. The summit's stone firetower, the trail, and the picnic shelter at the trailhead were constructed in the 1930s by the Civilian Conservation Corps (CCC), a government work program during the 1930s.

The second largest contiguous landholding by the State of Vermont, Groton State Forest is a scenic wilderness. Exposed mountain peaks in the forest display a granite bedrock similar to that of New Hampshire's White Mountains. Because the gravel, sand, silt, and numerous boulders left by the last glacier make the land unsuitable for farming, the forest has been primarily used for intensive logging.

This forested wilderness supports a variety of wildlife, including black bear, moose, deer, grouse, mink, beaver, otter, fisher, loons, herons, and many other species. The Forest also provides a variety of recreational activities, including an extensive network of hiking trails, a lake and ponds for boating and swimming, several picnic areas, and winter cross-country skiing and snowmobile trails.

To reach the trail drive north on US 2 from Marshfield Village (0.0) to the junction of VT 232 at 1.0 mile. Turn east on VT 232 and drive past the New Discovery Campground entrance at 5.3 miles. Continue beyond this entrance to a left turn marked by an Owl's Head sign at 6.6 miles. Turn left and follow this steep gravel road to the parking lot and picnic pavilion at 7.6 miles.

From the parking lot, turn right and walk to the picnic pavilion, where a signboard describes summer activities and programs, as well as hiking opportunities in the park. Take a moment to enjoy the view of Kettle Pond seen from the picnic pavilion overlook.

The trail begins behind the picnic shelter and approaches the outhouses visible from the parking lot. Turn right on the main trail and begin a very gradual hike through mixed hardwoods up the first set of CCC constructed steps. You soon reach another set of steps, as the trail bears left and begins a series of short switchbacks. Be sure to avoid all unblazed side trails and take time to notice the extensive CCC rock work.

At 0.25 mile you reach the top of Owl's Head and the octagonal stone firetower. A rock outcrop beyond the tower provides fantastic views of Groton State

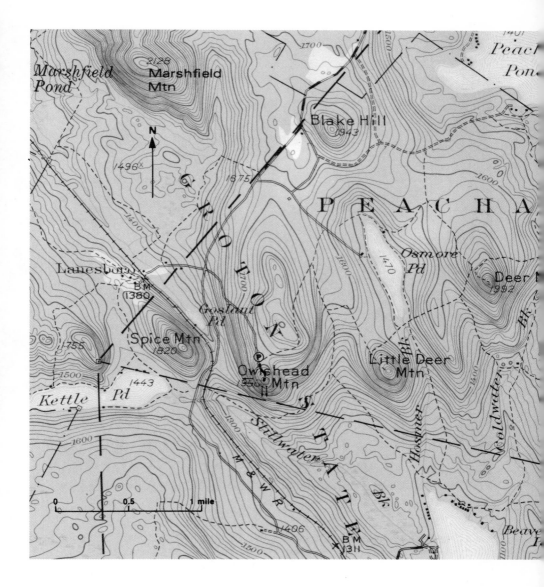

Park. Visible to the right is Kettle Pond, and to the left is Osmore Pond surrounded by Big Deer and Little Deer Mountains. To the southeast are approximately 850 contiguous acres of mature paper birch, red maple, and aspen, the result of intense fires around the turn of the century. This area is logged during the summer to disturb the soil enough to create an ideal seed-bed for the favored species of paper and yellow birch. Directly south is a 200-acre northern hardwood stand being regenerated to encourage aspen reproduction. Buds of

Fire tower on Owl's Head summit

mature male aspen trees are a highly preferred winter food source for ruffed grouse.

Take a short spur that leads north to another view of Osmore Pond. Hike back down the same trail to your car.

10

Mount Olga

Total distance: 1.4-mile loop
Hiking time: 1.5 hours
Vertical rise: 500 feet
Rating: Easy to moderate
Map: USGS Wilmington

The trail up Mount Olga is located in Molly Stark State Park, 3.4 miles east of Wilmington on VT 9. Molly Stark State Park was named after the wife of General John Stark. During the Revolutionary War in 1777, the general sent Molly

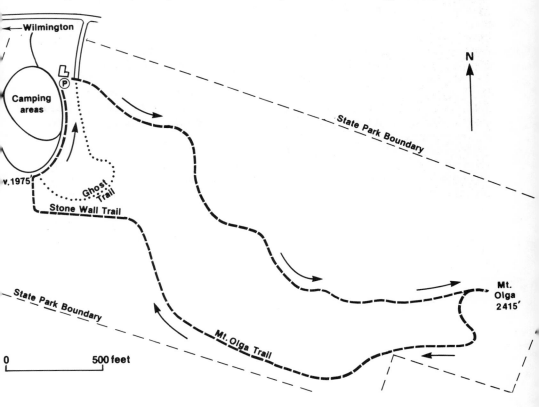

a message asking her to "send every man from the farm that will come and let the haying go." Molly organized their farm men and, along with two hundred other men, went to the general's aid. After the Battle of Bennington, General Stark returned home with one of the six brass cannons captured from the British as a token of gratitude to Molly.

This park, one of the smaller ones in the state park system, is a beautiful place to picnic or camp. Ample parking for cars is available. A day use fee is charged. You may want to pick up the free park brochure "Hiking Trail to Mount Olga" before beginning your hike.

The trail begins on the east side of the park road opposite the caretaker's home, next to the park entrance building. A sign indicates a distance of 0.7 mile to the firetower. Follow the blue-blazed trail down a short embankment on steps, across a small wooden bridge over a stream, and up through a stately spruce forest. The wide trail is covered with a soft carpet of needles. You soon cross over an old stone wall and continue your ascent to a left arrow. Turn left, pass among boulders and ferns, and then cross the remains of another low stone wall.

Climb again on moderate grades, until you reach a boulder and a rough barked maple tree growing on the left side of the trail. This tree has four distinct large trunks and several smaller four foot trees growing out of the crotch of the tree. The trail narrows, becomes steeper, and at 0.6 mile reaches a junction on the right. From the junction, the trail bears left and steeply ascends to the 2,415-foot wooded summit with a firetower, three old buildings, and a radio relay tower.

The summit was established as a fire lookout, with a wooden tower, in the early 1930s. In 1949–50 the wooden tower was removed and the steel tower from Bald Mountain in Townshend was transferred to Mount Olga. This tower, which is still standing, was abandoned as a fire lookout in the 1970s. Climb the firetower for a beautiful 360-degree panoramic view of southern Vermont, including Haystack Mountain, Mount Snow, and the Harriman Reservoir. You can also see into northwestern Massachusetts.

Return to the trail junction, turn left on the return loop, and descend on easy grades through numerous rock outcrops. Swinging right, you approach the park boundary, marked by red tape on the trees. Continue through a mixed forest on easy grades, between giant boulders and ledges, and across a wet area on planks. You reach the Ghost Trail junction at 1.3 miles. Continue downhill on the Stone Wall Trail, parallel to an old stone wall, through overgrown pasture land which is sometimes quite wet. The old stone wall and trail soon turn right and reach the campground road near campsite #10. Turn right and follow the road back to your car at 1.4 miles.

11

Robert Frost Trail

Total distance: 1 mile
Hiking time: 1 hour
Vertical rise: 120 feet
Rating: Easy
Map: GMNF 7.5' East Middlebury

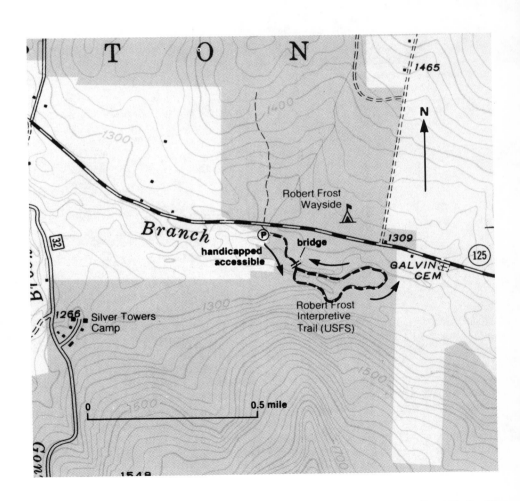

Handicapped accessible portion of Robert Frost Trail

Robert Front spent twenty-three summers in the Ripton area in a small cabin.
This trail, constructed in 1976 by the
Youth Conservation Corps, commemorates his poetry. Several of Frost's
poems are mounted on plaques along
the loop trail, and various signs describe
the natural environment. You may also
wish to stop at the Robert Frost Wayside
Recreation Area with picnic tables and
information boards 0.2 mile east of the
trailhead on VT 125.

The trail is located 2.1 miles east of
Ripton, or 9.8 miles from Hancock, on
the south side of VT 125. There is a
United States Forest Service (USFS) sign
at the trailhead parking area for ten to
twenty cars. An outhouse is provided. A
trail map signboard at the parking area
shows the location of the trail system. A
handicapped accessible trail loop is included at the beginning of the trail
system.

From the signboard, bear left and follow the gravel path past a sign which
lists significant dates and facts about

Robert Frost. You soon reach a junction,
where you bear left and cross the south
branch of the Middlebury River on a
bridge. After the bridge, turn right and
ascend to a softwood grove overlooking
the river. Here, the trail swings left and
follows easy grades through the forest.
Signs along the way identify many of the
trees and plants.

At 0.5 mile you enter an open
meadow and reach a bench. A sign
provides profiles of the area mountains,
including Firetower Hill, Bread Loaf
Mountain, Battell Mountain, Kirby Mountain, and Burnt Hills. The trail swings left
through the meadow and reaches a
bench overlooking the river. Prescribed
burning is used to keep the meadow
open and encourage the growth of blueberries and huckleberries.

The trail parallels the river, enters the
woods, and returns to the bridge. At the
"Y," bear left to cross a large wooden
bridge over a swamp. Then, turn right
and hike back to the parking area.

Southern Vermont

12

Flood Dam

Total distance: 4.6 miles
Hiking time: 2 hours
Vertical rise: 580 feet
Rating: Easy
Map: USGS 7.5' Mount Snow

This scenic hike crosses the Deerfield River on a suspension bridge and continues over rolling easy terrain to an old dam and pond. The two area suspension bridges were built in the late 1970s by the New England Power Company. The dam was originally a sluice dam for logs. The trail is located on New England Power Company land and no camping is allowed.

To reach the trail, drive 1.5 miles east on VT 9 from the intersection of VT 9 and VT 8. Turn left (north) on the New England Power Company Road. At 3.6 miles the trailhead is marked with a signpost and double diagonal yellow slashes. Roadside parking is available for approximately five cars.

From the signboard and post with two yellow slashes, descend and cross the Deerfield River on a suspension bridge. Cross the bridge one hiker at a time, as the bridge swings quite a bit with each step. The bridge's stone abutments are the remnants of an old road bridge. Continue your hike along an old roadway to a fork where the double yellow-blazed East Branch Trail goes right and you turn left on the single yellow-blazed Flood Dam Trail. Follow an old stone wall along the sometimes brushy trail to

an overgrown clearing. The apple trees and old wall indicate that the land was once pasture. Descend through softwoods and enter another overgrown clearing. Blueberries can be found in season along the trail.

Return to the woods and hike along the Deerfield River at 0.4 mile. As you reach the river, there is a spur trail to the left and a long cable around a tree. Perhaps the cable was part of a former river crossing.

Make a sharp right, pass through some softwoods, and ascend the hillside through mixed hardwoods. The trail becomes quite rocky and wet, but is drier as it levels and enters a mature hardwood forest at 1.2 miles. This forest is very colorful during fall foliage. Descend gradually, then more steeply, as you pass two old beaver ponds. Continue your descent along a small valley and veer right at 1.7 miles across a small brook. This portion of the trail is wet with slippery rocks and roots, so please watch your step. Hike along a small brook and, as you begin to see more light ahead through the trees, bear right on an abandoned railroad bed above the old flood dam. The railroad was built in the 1800s when the area was logged.

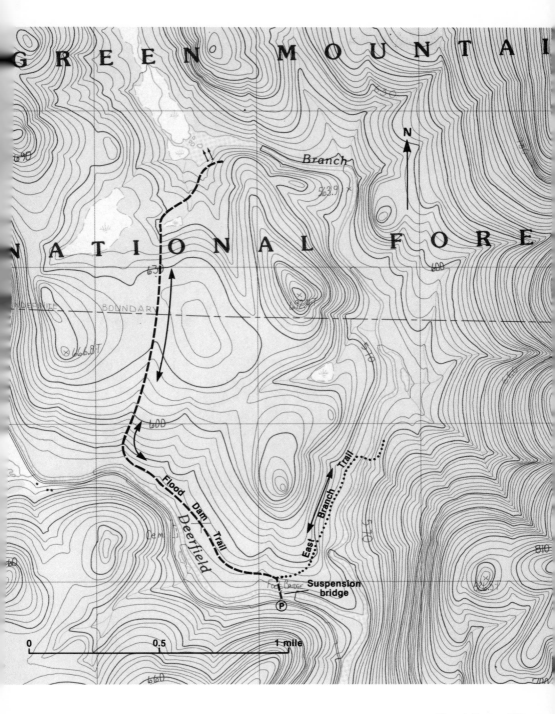

GREEN MOUNTAI

N

Branch

NATIONAL FORE

BOUNDARY

Flood Dam Trail

Deerfield

East Branch Trail

Suspension bridge

Foot Bridge

P

0   0.5   1 mile

Bridge across Deerfield River on Flood Dam Trail

The trail follows along the pond through dense young softwoods and ends at 2.3 miles in a clearing which overlooks the pond and a picnic area. Just ahead, you can see the rapids where the pond cascades over the remains of the old flood dam. Steel pins can still be seen in the old dam timbers.

Stop at the picnic table to rest, eat lunch, and enjoy the view across the pond before your return trip back the same trail. Before you leave, be sure to check for raspberries (in season) which grow behind the table. They make a delicious snack.

13

Haystack Mountain

Total distance: 4.8 miles
Hiking time: 3 hours
Vertical rise: 1,020 feet
Rating: Moderate
Map: USGS 7.5' Mount Snow

Rock outcroppings on the summit of Haystack Mountain provide beautiful views of southern Vermont and southwest New Hampshire.

Care is needed to find the trailhead, which is located in the Chimney Hills development northwest of Wilmington. From the traffic light in Wilmington (0.0), drive 1.1 miles west on VT 9. Turn right (north) on the Haystack Road and at 1.4 miles bear right, continuing to follow the paved Haystack Road. At 2.35 miles you reach an intersection where you turn left and follow the sign for the Clubhouse and Chimney Hill Road. At the next intersection, at 2.5 miles, turn right on the dirt Binney Brook Road. Bear left at the next three intersections. At 3.5 miles, turn right on the Upper Dam Road. Continue for a short distance on this road to a left turn at 3.6 miles. At 3.8 miles you reach the trailhead, marked on the right with an orange arrow pointing up the trail. Parking for about five cars is available along the road. Please do not block driveways or park on private property.

The trail, which follows an old road on easy to moderate grades, is sporadically marked with blue plastic diamonds. At the beginning of the trail, a yellow gate blocks vehicles from driving up the road. Watch on the left for Binney Brook, which is the outlet for Haystack and Crystal Ponds, and a galvanized spring pipe visible across the brook. At 0.75 mile the trail leaves the old road, which continues about one and a half miles to Crystal and Haystack Ponds. The trail turns left, and follows the Deerfield Ridge Trail, which is used extensively in the winter by snowmobilers and cross-country skiers. This section is marked for snowmobile use with orange blazes.

At 1.1 miles the trail turns right at a prominent orange arrow. Look for chipmunks and squirrels in the beech stand. The trail now climbs more gradually along the ridge. At 1.6 miles you reach a small promontory with Haystack Mountain visible straight ahead. You soon pass through a hemlock stand with views through the trees to the west. Bear right and continue to climb north along the ridge with unobstructed views to the west. Enter a boggy section, before gradually climbing through an evergreen stand. Enjoy the fresh balsam scent!

As the trail descends and skirts the southwestern edge of the mountain, you

View from Haystack Mountain

pass between two rock outcrops. Just beyond the rocks, you reach the intersection of the trail to Haystack Mountain. Turn right on this trail and ascend along the densely forested summit ridge until you reach a trail junction at 2.2 miles. Bear left and continue along the blue-blazed trail which ascends to another junction. Bear left again to the wooded summit at 2.4 miles. (Remember to note where the trail enters the summit.)

Two rock outcrops provide views to the north of Haystack Pond, the Haystack Mountain Ski Area, and the summit of Mount Snow. To the south you can see the Harriman Reservoir; to the southwest, Mount Greylock, the highest mountain in Massachusetts; to the west, the firetower on the summit of Glastenbury Mountain; and, to the east, Monadnock Mountain in New Hampshire.

After enjoying the view, hike back down the same trail to return to your car.

14

Prospect Rock (Manchester)

Total distance: 3 miles
Hiking time: 2.5 hours
Vertical rise: 1,100 feet
Rating: Strenuous
Map: USGS 7.5' Manchester

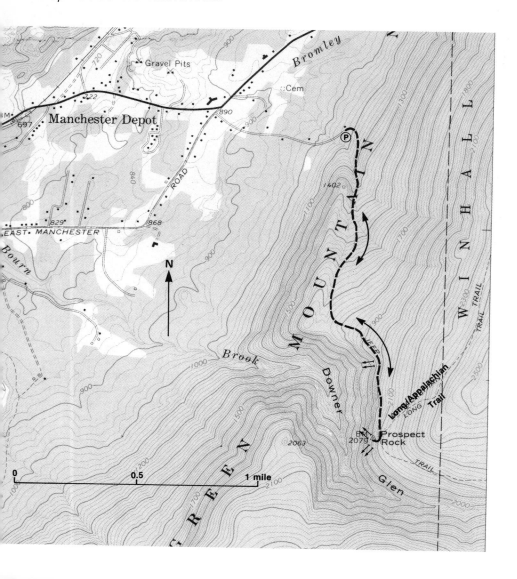

Prospect Rock (Manchester)

To reach the trail begin at the junction of VT 11, VT 30 and US 7 (0.0) about 1 mile east of Manchester. Drive east on VT 11 and VT 30 for 0.5 mile to the junction of the East Manchester Road on your right. Take a right on East Manchester Road and continue to Rootville Road at 0.55 mile. Take a left on this road to the white water tower on the right and a small gravel driveway and a house. Park near the water tower; there is parking for five cars at 1.05 miles, just before the No Parking signs. Do not block the road and do not park near or drive past the signs.

Begin your hike up the unmaintained "Old Rootville Road" to a Green Mountain National Forest signboard on the right. Continue on the moderately graded old road up the side of the mountain and listen to the brook flowing on your right. You pass a spur trail, the small brook comes into view on the right, and the old road ascends more steeply up the mountain.

This hike is wonderful in the fall because of the many different trees: white and yellow birch, maple, oak, and spruce. At 0.3 mile the road crosses the brook on an old culvert, and is soon met by another small brook on the right. Continue to crisscross the brook until you reach a spring box on the left, where the brook turns to the left away from the road. The road is quite washed out and rocky in this section, with water sometimes in the road. After climbing to another spring at 0.8 mile, leave the sound of the brooks behind and enjoy a deep quiet interrupted only by birds and chipmunks.

The old road soon levels off and passes through a beautiful birch stand filled with sunlight, on days when clouds don't intercede. The trail eventually starts climbing again with a steep drop off to the right and views of Downer Glen. At this point, the road is carved out of the side of the mountain, and levels off before climbing on easier grades. Manchester Center and Mount Equinox can be seen through the trees.

At 1.5 miles you reach a junction where the white-blazed Long Trail branches off to the left and goes north to Spruce Peak and Bromley Mountain. Continue straight a few more feet on the old road to a spur trail on the right, which leads about 200 feet east to Prospect Rock.

From the Rock, high above Downer Glen, you can see the highway and Manchester Center. To the northwest, up the valley, is Dorset. Mount Aeolus is to the right of the valley and Mount Equinox, with its four windmills on the left of its summit, can be seen to the left of the valley.

After enjoying the views, return along the same trails.

15

Harmon Hill

Total distance: 3.4 miles
Hiking time: 3 hours
Vertical rise: 1,265 feet
Rating: Moderate
Maps: GMNF Woodford, Bennington, Pownal, Stamford

Trail up Harmon Hill

This hike features an elaborate set of stone steps that ascend from the VT 9 valley, and extensive views of Bennington and the Taconic Mountain Range. You also see the monument which commemorates the August 16, 1777, Battle of Bennington.

The trailhead is located at the Long Trail/Appalachian Trail (LT/AT) parking lot on the north side VT 9, 4.5 miles east of Bennington. Parking for twenty-five or more cars is available in this lot on the north side of the highway. A Green Mountain National Forest sign marks the trailhead on the south side of VT 9.

Begin your hike heading south across the road from the parking lot on the white-blazed LT/AT. The trail enters the woods at a double-blaze, turns right, and begins a long steep ascent up stone steps. Climb quickly to a moss-covered boulder and outcrop, then traverse the first level section before climbing more stone steps. The road can be seen below you as you gain elevation. At 0.2 mile you begin a series of long switchbacks, moving from one set of steps to another, as you ascend out of the valley.

Light through the trees indicates the climb is almost finished, as you near the top of the ridge. At 0.6 mile the trail levels and descends slightly through a forest of primarily maple, birch and oak trees. This area provides a welcome contrast to the climb you just completed. You soon cross a tiny brook and enter a fern meadow. As you return to the forest, you reach a long set of puncheon at 1.0 mile. Puncheon are small wooden bridges of one or more log or board planks held off the ground on sills. Cross another wet area on puncheon and stones, and ascend through a darker, denser woods.

At 1.5 miles you come to another fern meadow with sunlight filtering through the trees. Soon the meadow opens up even more and Bald Mountain ridge can be seen to the northwest. Raspberries growing along the trail should be ripe in late July. You pass through tall ferns before you reach the 2,325-foot summit at 1.7 miles. Spur trails lead to views of Bennington, the Monument, the Taconics, and Mount Anthony. The large meadow is kept open through the use of controlled burns by the United States Forest Service.

To return to your car, follow the same trail. Be careful through the wet areas and on the steps, which are almost as difficult to descend as they are to ascend.

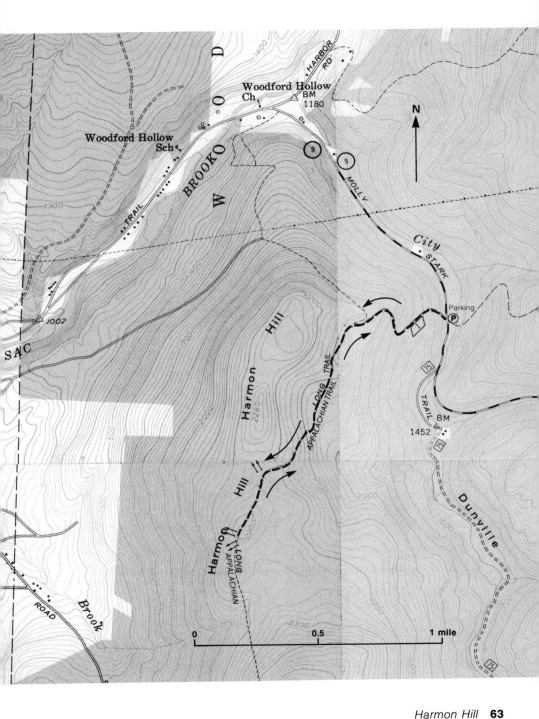

N

Woodford Hollow
Ch
BM
1180

Woodford Hollow Sch

BROOKO W

TRAIL

1300

1002

SAC

Harmon Hill

Hill

LONG TRAIL

APPALACHIAN TRAIL

Harmon Hill

LONG APPALACHIAN

HARBOR RD

MOLLY

City

STARK

Parking
P

75

TRAIL
BM
1452
75

Dunville

75

ROAD

Brook

| 0 | 0.5 | 1 mile |

16

Stratton Mountain

Total distance: 9-mile loop
Hiking time: 7 hours
Vertical rise: 1,910 feet
Rating: Moderately strenuous
Map: GMNF Londonderry SW

This long, beautiful hike has several scenic overlooks of Somerset Reservoir and Stratton Pond, as well as nice views from the summit tower. You can also hike out and back the same trail in 6.8 miles for a shorter trip.

Stratton Mountain played an important role in the conception of both the Long Trail and the Appalachian Trail. On Stratton Mountain in 1909, James P. Taylor thought about a "long trail" which would link the summits of the Green Mountains. Several years later on the same mountain, Benton MacKaye was inspired to develop an entire trail system in the northeast along the Appalachian Mountains from Georgia to Maine.

To reach the trail, take VT 100 to the junction of the Arlington-West Wardsboro Road (or Kelley Stand Road) in West Wardsboro (0.0). Drive 7.1 miles west on the Arlington-West Wardsboro Road to the Long Trail/Appalachian (LT/AT) parking lot on the north side of the road. There is parking space for eight to ten cars. A United States Forest Service (USFS) sign marks the trailhead.

Begin your hike north along the white-blazed LT/AT up the bank behind the parking area. You quickly enter the woods and climb onto a small knob. Nu-

merous old logging roads intersect the trail and, at times, you follow them for a short distance. You cross several wet areas on puncheon, which are small wooden bridges of one or more log or board planks held off the ground on sills. At 0.7 mile you come to a beaver dam, and hike uphill through a mixed hard and softwood forest. At 1.1 miles you pass by an old farm site with apple trees, a stone wall, and several foundations. Hike through an overgrown pasture, and continue through a birch stand. Cross the gated, gravel USFS Road-FR 341 at 1.3 miles. Make a note of this junction, since you will be completing your return loop along this road.

Beyond the road, the trail ascends, crosses a brook, and passes by several old logging roads. The trail gets steeper and reaches a shelf at 1.7 miles. Continue your steep ascent over uneven rocks up the ridge through a mixed hardwood forest with numerous birches. At 2.5 miles you intersect the old "Stratton Mountain Trail."

In 1986, after years of negotiation with the property owner, International Paper Company, the USFS obtained funding to purchase the western slope of Stratton Mountain. In the mid-1980s, Vermont's

Mount Snow and Somerset Reservoir from Stratton Mountain

congressional delegation worked to obtain federal monies for this acquisition. They were successful, but the Gramm-Rudman-Hollings deficit-reduction law delayed the funds. In 1985, The Nature Conservancy acquired 12,000 acres, including the summit, and held it in trust, until the Forest Service received the allocated money. The relocation, which involved 8.7 miles of new trail, was finally completed in 1989.

Continue your hike parallel to the ridgeline, as the trail becomes less steep. Climb again along several switchbacks, pass among higher elevation spruce and birch, and come to a view

at 2.75 miles of Somerset Reservoir and Mount Snow. Beyond the overlook, ascend past a piped spring on the left. You now hike through primarily balsam fir trees along several switchbacks, until you reach the firetower at 3.4 miles.

Stratton Mountain was one of the earliest firetower sites in Vermont. A steel tower was constructed in 1914. In the early 1930s, a new cabin and steel lookout tower were built by the Civilian Conservation Corps, a government work program. This tower, abandoned as a firetower around 1980, was repainted and repaired by the USFS in 1988. The tower, the only one remaining on USFS

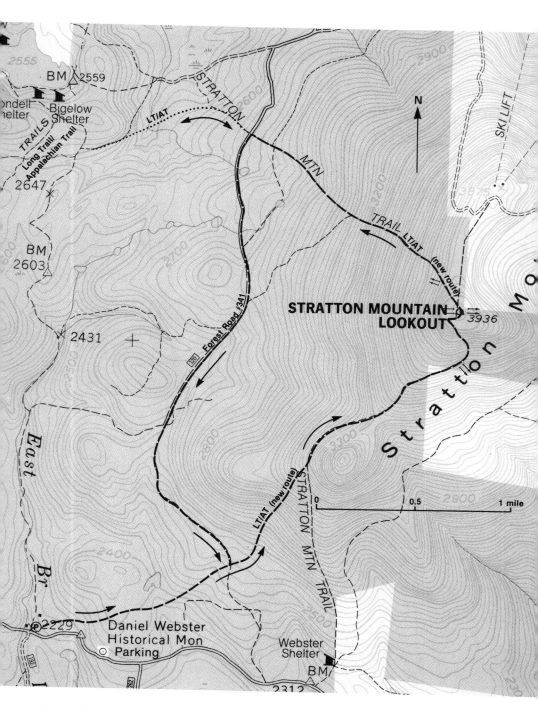

Vermont lands, was nominated to the National Register of Historic Places in 1989.

Please note that a Ranger-Naturalist, supported by the Green Mountain Club, Appalachian Trail Conference, and the Green Mountain National Forest, lives in the cabin and is stationed on the summit during hiking season. No camping is permitted on the summit.

From the tower you can enjoy spectacular views: to the south, Somerset Reservoir and Mount Snow; to the southwest, Glastenbury Mountain; to the west, Mount Equinox and the Taconic Mountain Range; to the northeast, Mount Ascutney; and, to the southeast, Mount Monadnock.

Unless you decide to take the shorter 6.8 mile route back down the same trail to your car, continue north on the LT/AT along the summit ridge and begin to descend. At 3.5 miles you reach an overlook of Stratton Pond with Mount Equinox in the distance. In the next section, the trail utilizes stone steps, waterbars, and turnpiking to cross a wet area. Turnpiking is a raised trailbed formed by placing logs on either side of the trail and filling between them with dirt and gravel. Waterbars are a drainage system of log or rock construction. They are the best defense against trail erosion. A waterbar is composed of three parts: the bar, built of log or rock; the apron, a shallow slope to funnel water to the bar and ditch; and the ditch, which carries water off the trail.

At 4.0 miles you steeply descend over rocks and roots in the trail, and begin a series of long switchbacks through a softwood forest. As the trail passes through mixed hardwoods, you continue your descent and cross a small brook at 4.7 miles. The trail soon intersects several old logging roads, steeply descends for a short distance, and crosses a wet area on puncheon.

After a more moderate descent, you reach the gravel FR 341 at 5.1 miles. The LT/AT goes one mile straight ahead to Stratton Pond. You turn left and follow the USFS road to the LT/AT intersection (at 7.6 miles), which you passed at the beginning of your hike. Hike the LT/AT south back down the trail to your car at 9 miles.

17

Stratton Pond

Total distance: 7.8 miles
Hiking time: 5 hours
Vertical rise: 660 feet
Rating: Moderate
Map: GMNF Londonderry SW

This long, but almost level hike leads to Stratton Pond, which is located in the 15,680-acre Lye Brook Wilderness. There are few trails through this heavily forested wilderness, but several lakes, streams, and bogs dot the landscape. The Wilderness contains beautiful waterfalls and meadows, as well as the remnants of old logging railroads and sawmills. "The Burning," the site of a large fire around the turn of the century, is located in the western portion of the Wilderness. It is a popular spot for wildlife such as wild turkey, whitetail deer, and black bear.

The trail is located on the north side of the Arlington-West Wardsboro Road (also known as the Kelley Stand Road). From VT 100 in West Wardsboro (0.0), drive 8.2 miles west on the Arlington-West Wardsboro Road to the intersection of United States Forest Service (USFS) Road-FR 71. A parking lot on FR 71 just south of the intersection has space for ten to fifteen cars. A wooden USFS sign and information board mark the trailhead.

This blue-blazed trail follows the former route of the Long Trail/Appalachian Trail (LT/AT). Note the extensive trailwork, including waterbars, puncheon,

and turnpiking (see the previous trail description for more on these).

Begin your hike across puncheon and over turnpiking through a young beech and softwood forest. The trail ascends slightly and crosses several wet areas on puncheon, which resemble a boardwalk through the woods. At 1.0 mile you cross an old red-blazed property line, descend slightly through white birches, and come to an open area with ferns. Descend again at 1.5 miles on puncheon across another wet area and enter a birch forest. This area is quite beautiful on a sunny day, with sunlight filtering through the birch trees.

At 2.3 miles you cross an old road, enter a dark, dense softwood forest, and climb five wooden steps to return to a sunnier, more open hardwood forest. As you begin a gradual ascent, notice the large stumps that indicate the size of the trees once logged in this area. Cross another wet area on puncheon and look on your right for a large birch with roots engulfing a boulder. Continue your hike through a small softwood forest, across more puncheon, and past a large moss-covered boulder.

At 3.8 miles you cross a small brook on stepping stones. Look for a double-

N

WILDERNES

TRATION

BROOK

TRAIL

7 × BROOK

LYE BROOK

Stratton View
Shelter

2442

**Stratton
Pond**

2555

BM 2559

LT/AT

STRATTON

Vondell
Shelter

Bigelow
Shelter

LT/AT

2647 ×

BM
2603 △

2431 ×

East

Br.

Stratton Pond Trail

2500

Black

71A

P Parking

FH6

Brook

Dee

2229 ×

Daniel Webster
Historical Mon
⊙ Parking

0   0.5   1 mile

G R E E N

Stratton Pond

blaze, where you turn left and descend a rocky, wet, old logging road to the junction of the LT/AT. A USFS sign indicates that Stratton Mountain is 2.6 miles from this junction.

Follow the LT/AT north to the shore of Stratton Pond. Stratton Pond, the largest body of water on the Long Trail, has the most overnight use of any location on the trail. There are over 2,000 overnight hikers at the pond between Memorial Day and Columbus Day. The use is concentrated along the pond's shoreline, which is particularly prone to damage. The pond, where you can swim and fish, is 30 feet deep at the deepest point, and an average of 10 feet deep overall. Most of the pond and surrounding lands were acquired by the USFS in 1985. A Green Mountain Club Caretaker is stationed at the site during the hiking season to assist hikers and maintain the trails and shelters. Please follow the caretaker's instructions to help protect this valuable natural area.

An information board at the pond describes a 1.4 mile loop trail around the pond which you may wish to explore if you have time. After exploring the pond area, return via the same trails on which you set out.

18

Griffith Lake and Baker Peak

Total distance: 8.9 miles
Hiking time: 5 hours
Vertical rise: 2,340 feet
Rating: Strenuous
Map: GMNF Wallingford NW

The first 3.5 miles of this strenuous hike follow the Lake Trail over an old road. The road was once a carriage road to the Griffith Lake House, a club house near the summit of Baker Peak owned by Silas L. Griffith. The foundation of the house can still be seen on the west shore of the lake. Silas Griffith, Vermont's first millionaire, lived in Danby and operated a sawmill which became known as the town of Griffith.

To reach the trail, drive 2.2 miles south of Danby (0.0) on US 7 to a small road on the left (east) side of US 7. Turn left on the road and cross a set of railroad tracks. The road passes a small cemetery on the right, heads toward the ridge, swings right, and at 2.7 miles reaches a small parking lot for five to six cars on the left.

The trail starts at the right rear corner of the lot and ascends on easy grades. You soon cross a brook, hike parallel to the brook, and cross two smaller brooks. At 0.75 mile the old roadway widens through a hemlock grove, but quickly narrows and begins a sweeping switchback to the left, until you reach a United States Forest Service (USFS) No Vehicles sign. Continue climbing past a steep ledge on your right. (Imagine the

labor required to construct the old road.) At 1.6 miles you cross a rock slab on a narrow bridge. Look below in the rock for the metal pins which once held the carriage road bridge in place. A notch in the mountain ridge is visible ahead, as the trail swings right. The trail gets steeper, as you follow along McGinn Brook flowing out of the valley. At 2.0 miles you reach the junction of the Baker Peak Trail, on which you will return.

The Lake Trail bears right, continues upstream on easy grades, and crosses a brook, as the trail becomes quite wet and rocky. Numerous small brooks cross the trail in this section. The trail bears right into the woods to avoid a very wet part of the old roadway. You soon return to the old road and pass through a maple forest on easy grades. The trail leaves the road at an obscure junction, crests a small knob, and reaches the LT/AT junction at 3.5 miles.

Turn right and follow the white-blazed LT/AT to Griffith Lake. A high, sixteen-acre mountain lake, Griffith Lake was originally called Buffum Pond. This warm water lake averages ten feet deep, and although stocked with brook trout, it is not a particularly good fishing

Danby

662

N

South Buckl
P

Lost P

Shelter

WILDERNESS

2850

Baker
Peak

Elbow
Swamp

BAKER PEAK TRAIL

Long and Appalachian Trails

GREEN

South End

Cem

McGinn

Bk

Lake Trail

LAKE TRAIL

Parking

LAKE TRAIL

Lake Trail

LAKE TRAIL

OLD JQB

ROCK'S CORRIDOR

Long
Hole

BRANCH

Griffith
Lake

TERRA

Otter

FOR NATL FOR BDY

Peru Peak
Shelter

NATI

0   0.5   1 mile

View of Route 7 from Baker Peak

site. All camping at the lake is restricted to designated sites within 200 feet of the shore. A Green Mountain Club Caretaker is stationed at the lake during hiking season. A small fee is charged for overnight use.

After enjoying the lake, return to the trail junction at 3.7 miles and follow the LT/AT north along a relatively level grade to Baker Peak. From the junction, hike up, down, and over wet areas on puncheon, until you reach a large boulder. Puncheon are small wooden bridges of one or more log or board planks held off the ground on sills. Continue over several rock shelves with occasional views along the birch lined hillside. At 5.4 miles you reach the Baker Peak Trail Junction. Follow the LT/AT up the exposed rock slab to the summit. Be very careful of your footing along the slab. From the summit of Baker Peak you have great views of

Dorset Peak directly across the valley; Mount Equinox and the Stratton Mountain firetower to the south; Pico and Killington peaks to the north; and the Otter Creek meandering through the narrow US 7 valley below.

From the summit, return to the junction and steeply descend the ridge along the blue-blazed Baker Peak Trail. You quickly reach an overlook, called "Quarry View," of the stone quarries on Dorset Peak. After enjoying the view, descend more gradually along a rock outcrop through mixed hardwoods. The trail soon bears right and begins a steep descent, until you enter a fern-filled maple forest where the trail levels slightly. The trail now resembles an old road. You begin to hear water as you reach the Lake Trail Junction at 6.9 miles. Turn right, cross the brook, and return along the old carriage road to your car at 8.9 miles.

Bald Mountain

Total distance: 3.5-mile loop
Hiking time: 3 hours
Vertical rise: 1,100 feet
Rating: Moderate ascent/strenuous descent
Map: USGS 15' Saxtons River

View from Bald Mountain with Mount Monadnock in the distance

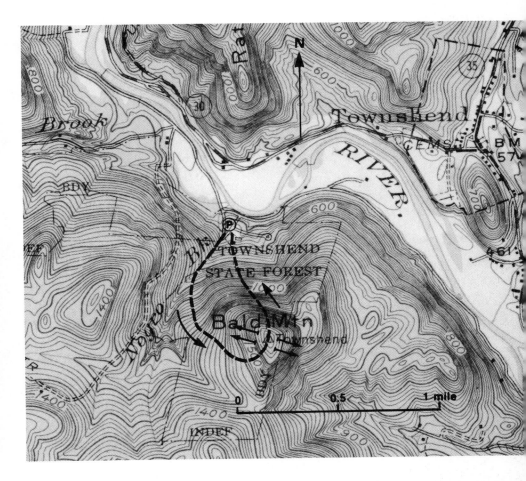

Bald Mountain, located in Townshend State Forest, offers excellent views of the surrounding area. The Forest is located next to Townshend State Park where you can swim and picnic before or after your hike. On your way to the trail, you pass the Scott Covered Bridge which spans the West River. The bridge, built in 1870, is 165.7 feet long—the longest single span covered bridge in Vermont.

To reach the Townshend State Forest, drive 2.0 miles north of Townshend Village on VT 30 to the Townshend Dam.

Turn left (west) and cross the spillway on a narrow bridge. Just past the dam and recreation access (0.0), the road reaches a "T" at 0.2 mile. Turn left and pass the Scott Covered Bridge at 0.8 mile. Bear right at the bridge and continue parallel to the West River, until you reach the Park entrance at 1.4 miles. Parking is available in a small lot on the right just before the Park building. Walk to the building, where a day use fee is charged.

Begin your hike across the road, to the right of the park building. Descend on a short spur trail to campsite #25 where the trailhead is marked with a sign and very large blue blazes. Take the trail over a brook on a pole bridge, turn left, and follow the brook along an old road. Take time to enjoy the brook's pretty cascades and pools. The road climbs a steep bank away from the brook, but soon returns to cross the brook near a property line and an old bridge abutment. The trail bears left at an old road junction and ascends away from the brook. At 0.6 mile the trail bears right to avoid a logging area, then parallels and crosses a logging road. Ascend along the hillside, covered with small boulders, into an open softwood forest. The trail bears right and continues on easy grades through several wet areas.

At 1.1 miles you pass by a large boulder and cross a brook. An old road intersects the trail, which now follows the brook bed. Bear left off the old brook bed and enter an alder swamp. The trail begins to ascend along the hillside, which resembles an overgrown, old rocky pasture. Look for numerous oak trees. Continue on the steep but quite open trail to the 1,680-foot summit at 1.7 miles. A sign directs you to a southern view of Mount Monadnock in New Hampshire and the West River Valley below you. From the northern view you can see Stratton and Bromley Mountains. Between the two overlooks you can still see the foundation footings of an old firetower. A fire station was established on Bald Mountain in 1912. A steel tower was built on the summit in the early 1930s, but the tower was transferred to Mount Olga.

From the summit, take the blue-blazed trail to the right of the northern overlook. You enter the woods and rapidly descend through softwoods. Watch your footing in this difficult section. At 2.0 miles the trail bears right to avoid an eroded area and begins a steep sidehill traverse on a very narrow trail. Occasional views are possible of Townshend Reservoir below as the trail continues its descent and crosses a small brook. At 2.8 miles the trail bears left again, descends steeply, and then continues gently downhill through a nice maple grove lined with ferns. Another steep descent takes you to 3.3 miles, where the downgrade eases up; eventually you reach the campground road near a huge tree stump at campsite #6. Follow this road back to the parking area at 3.5 miles.

20

Mount Antone

Total distance: 5 miles
Hiking time: 3 hours
Vertical rise: 890 feet
Rating: Moderate
Map: USGS 7.5' Pawlet

View from Mount Antone

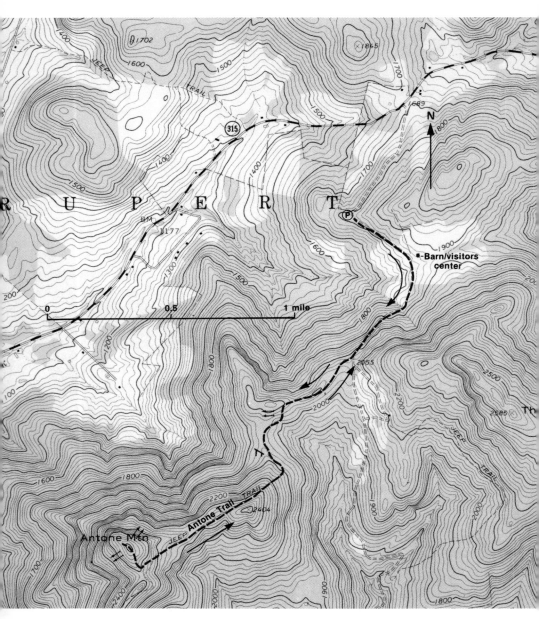

This hike follows only some of the twenty-six miles of trails at the Merck Forest and Farmland Center. The center is a nonprofit outdoor educational center which also contains a small diversified farm, fields, hardwood forests, and several small ponds and streams. The center offers a variety of educational programs, including astronomy, forest management, wildflower and bird identification, and low-impact camping.

The center can be reached from the junction of VT 315 and VT 30 in East Rupert (0.0). Take VT 315 west 2.4 miles to the height of land and a Merck Forest sign on your left. Turn left on the dirt road and continue to a gate and a ten-car parking area at 2.9 miles. A signboard at the gate includes area rules (no mountain bikes; no unleashed dogs), as well as trail maps that are available with a donation to help cover the center's expenses.

The unblazed trail, which follows old roads, starts from the gate. Follow the dirt road on level grades until you reach a field on the right. The caretaker's cabin, as well as other cabins for overnight use, are on the left. At the road fork ahead there are picnic tables, a barn, and a Visitor's Center. Take time to visit the center's interesting exhibits on area wildlife and forests.

Continue your hike on the Old Towne Road to the right at the fork. This road, the first one in Merck Forest, was built by Ebenezer Smith in 1781 to provide access between his home on the mountain and the town highway. The most recent roads are used for logging and sugaring, which help support the educational center. Old Towne Road passes several fields, descends for a short distance, and then ascends on easy grades. Enjoy the nice views to the north and northwest of New York's Adirondack Mountains.

Stay on the Old Towne Road through the Gallop Road intersection on the left, and then the Old McCormick Road intersection on the right at 0.5 mile. Hike up a short steep grade and pass a small clearing on the right as the road levels again. Make a left turn and come to a well-marked junction with the Lodge Road on the left and the Mount Antone Road on the right. Turn right on the Mount Antone Road along easy grades on top of the ridge, and then descend to Clark's Clearing at 1.3 miles. You pass the McCormick Road junction on the right and a small lean-to for firewood on the left. Look for berry bushes in two small clearings, where you can feast on ripe berries in late July while enjoying views of Mount Antone.

Follow the trail into the woods until you come to an overnight shelter and trail intersection. The Clark's Clearing Road bears left and a spur trail bears right. Continue to the south on the Mount Antone Road up a steep grade to the top of the ridge. The road levels and starts an easy, winding descent. At 1.9 miles you reach the Wade Lot Road junction on the left. Hike past the Lookout Road junction, again on the left, and climb the mountainside on moderate grades past the Beebe Pond Trail and Masters Mountain Trail junctions. The Mount Antone Trail continues up a steep grade to the 2,610-foot summit at 2.5 miles. There are views to the east and northeast of the Visitor Center's barn, Dorset Peak, Woodlawn Mountain, and the Pawlet area. A trail beyond the summit leads downhill to another lookout, with good views of the Adirondack Mountains, eastern New York, and the Rupert and Pawlet areas.

After enjoying the views, hike back to the summit and down the trail to the parking area at 5.0 miles.

21

Little Rock Pond/Green Mountain Trail

Total distance: 7 miles
Hiking time: 6-7 hours
Vertical rise: 960 feet
Rating: Moderately strenuous
Map: GMNF Wallingford NW and SW

This hike, which provides a nice variation from the usual "out and back" trail, allows you to enjoy both mountain trails and a beautiful pond. Leave a full day for this journey to give yourself adequate time to enjoy the pond, as well as some wonderful views.

To reach the trail, take VT 7 to the junction of VT 7 and United States Forest Service (USFS) Road-FR 10 (near the towns of Danby and Mount Tabor). Turn east on FR 10, also called the Danby-Landgrove Road (0.0), cross the railroad tracks, and go by the USFS Mount Tabor Work Center Sign. Follow the road uphill to 0.9 mile, where a sign indicates that you have entered the White Rocks National Recreational Area. At 2.7 miles you reach Big Branch Overlook. The road turns to dirt at 3.0 miles. You soon cross a bridge and reach the Long Trail parking area at 3.2 miles, where there is space for approximately twenty cars.

From the parking area, cross the road and follow the white-blazed Long Trail north to Little Rock Pond. The sign post at the trailhead indicates a distance of two miles to the pond, your first stop on this hike. The beginning of this trail, which starts as a gradual climb, is strewn with bricks and black soot from an old charcoal kiln. Enter some mixed hardwoods and start to leave the brook behind. You follow an old roadway parallel to the brook on the left, and soon cross the brook on a steel I-beam bridge at 0.6 mile.

The trail swings right after the bridge, and continues to follow, then crosses the brook. By 1.0 mile the brook is considerably smaller as you cross a wet area on puncheon, a small wooden bridge of one or more log or board planks held off the ground on sills. The trail then switches from a roadway into a more "rugged" trail with numerous slippery wet areas, so be sure to watch your step. At 1.8 miles you reach a spur trail on the right that goes to the Lula Tye Shelter. A sign at this junction says the pond is 0.2 mile farther along the Long Trail. The trail becomes very rocky during this next section, so be careful of your footing until you reach the south end of the pond at 2.0 miles.

Little Rock Pond, up to 60 feet deep in places, is one of the most popular day use areas and the highest overnight use area on the Long Trail. The pond, a good fishing spot, is annually stocked with brook trout. Beavers frequent the

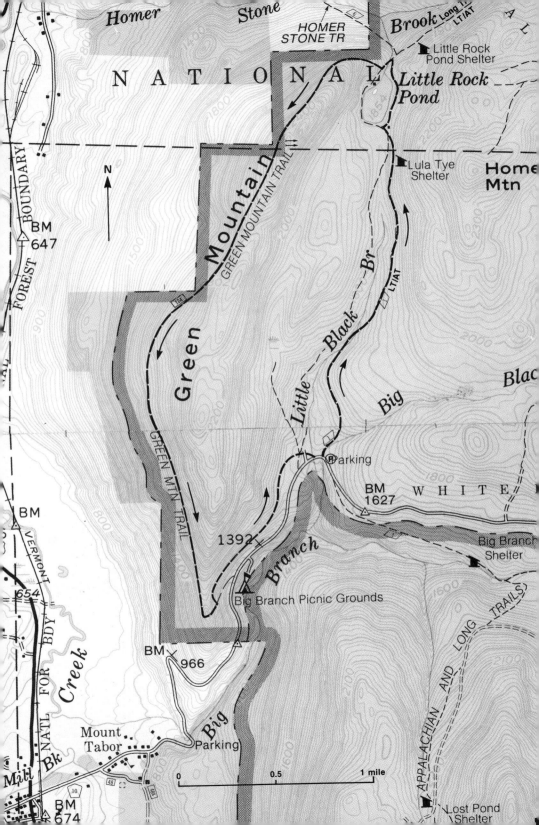

area, and moose have occasionally been sited along the pond shore. Careful management is required to preserve the area's nature beauty and fragile shoreline environment. Due to the area's popularity, a Green Mountain Club Caretaker is stationed at the site during the hiking season.

A signboard points out the trails around the pond and the campsites. As you follow the Long Trail around the pond, you soon cross a piped spring. At 2.4 miles you reach the north end of the pond. Continue north and cross a brook to the junction of the Green Mountain Trail and the Little Rock Pond Loop. The Long Trail continues straight ahead, but you turn left on the pond loop and Green Mountain Trail. A sign indicates a distance of 0.9 mile to the pond lookout and 4.5 miles back to the parking lot.

Ascend the trail to "Loop Junction" at 2.5 miles and turn right, away from the pond, on the blue-blazed Green Mountain Trail. Switchback up the ridge and climb up the edge of a pointed rock outcrop. Occasional views along the trail remind you how far you've climbed above the pond. At 3.0 miles you reach a ledge with views down to the pond. Return to a wooded ridge walk, climb over a steep rock face, and reach the "Pond View" junction. Hike straight ahead for 100 yards to spectacular views of the pond and valley below.

From the junction, the trail takes a sharp right into a spruce forest, with minor ascents and switchbacks. Pass through a series of rock shelves and, on the left at 3.7 miles, reach a short spur trail to a nice view. Descend the trail, which now resembles an old road, through some mixed hardwoods. The trail is quite wide in this section. The end of the first major descent is reached at 4.5 miles, where you turn left and continue through mature hardwoods. Be careful to watch for blazes in this area. Continue your descent until you cross a brook at 5.2 miles and enter a much younger hardwood forest. The trail climbs again, and then levels off. You soon reach a very unusual old road cut out of the hillside. Enjoy views of the valley along the road. As you cross a rock slide, take time to notice that the area uphill is predominantly hardwood, while the valley below is all softwood; the road forms the dividing line. The trail then swings around the edge of the ridge and you begin to hear Big Branch Brook.

At 6.4 miles you reach another trail junction, where you turn left to return to your car. The trail straight ahead leads to another parking lot and FR 10. As you turn left and return to the woods, you pass through some beech trees and ascend a small hill. Turn right and descend along an old road. At the bottom of the hill you begin to see FR 10 on the right as you cross a wet overgrown area parallel to the highway. At 7.0 miles you cross a gravel road, pass through another wet overgrown area, and descend to the road. Turn left and return to the parking lot.

22

Ascutney Mountain

Total distance: 6 miles
Hiking time: 4.5 hours
Vertical rise: 2,250 feet
Rating: Strenuous
Map: USGS 7.5' Mount Ascutney

Ascutney Mountain is an unusual quartz monadnock located near Windsor. The mountain's quartz syenite rock has withstood the erosion and glaciation that has worn away the softer rocks of the surrounding piedmont peneplain, an area near the foot of a mountain which has been almost reduced to a plain by erosion.

The first trail on Ascutney Mountain was opened in 1825. The mountain derives its name from the Abnaki words Cas-Cad-Nac, meaning "mountain of the rocky summit." In 1883, a summer-long forest fire burned away stretches of trail on the mountain. Great boulders lined the trails, and charred tree trunks and ash were everywhere. The Ascutney Mountain Association was formed in 1903 to relocate many of the damaged trails, rebuild the destroyed hut on top of the mountain, and to perpetually maintain the hut and trails.

In 1920, a ranger cabin and tower were constructed on the mountain. Around 1940, the Civilian Conservation Corps (CCC), a government work program, built a new steel tower which was abandoned as a firetower in the 1950s. The tower remained standing until the mid-1980s.

The building of a road in 1934 by the CCC, as well as the Great Hurricane of 1938, created so much debris and so many trail problems that little maintenance was done on the trails until 1966. In 1966, the Herbert Ogdens (junior and senior) located, cleared, blazed, signed, measured, and mapped the Windsor Trail. In 1967, the Ascutney Trails Association was formed to continue their work; it still maintains the trails on the mountain.

Because of several summit antennas, the summit is not as interesting as the west peak which is more secluded and used as a hang glider launching site.

To reach the trail, take Exit 8 (Ascutney) off I-91 to VT 131 west (0.0). Drive 3.3 miles to Cascade Falls Road and turn right (north). Bear left at the fork and continue to a right turn at 3.6 miles. Drive up the short steep hill to the fifteen-car parking lot and the Ascutney State Park information board. The trailhead and parking area were built in 1989 by the State of Vermont and the Ascutney Trails Association.

From the information board at the left rear end of the parking lot, take the blue-blazed Weathersfield Trail, which ascends some small log stairs and en-

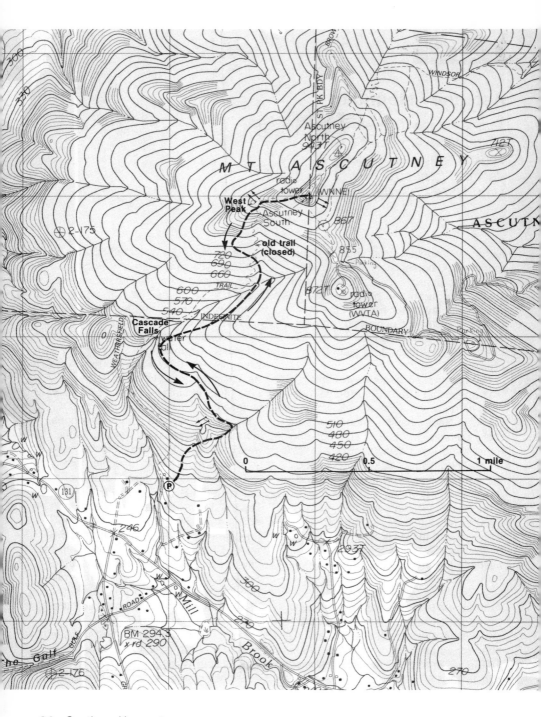

View from Mount Ascutney

ters the woods. Several property stakes line the trail. Swing right along easy grades and cross a small brook. The trail becomes rocky, ascends a steep gully along switchbacks, and crosses over Little Cascade Falls. Turn left, continue your ascent through a deep rock cleft, and hike out the other side on rock and log steps. Now on easier grades, pass several overlooks at 0.6 mile. The trail intersects an old road and enters a softwood forest. Descend to Crystal Cascade, then turn right, and ascend along the falls.

The geology of Crystal Cascade appears to be unique in Vermont. It is a rare example of a ring dike, formed by the upward flow of magma in a somewhat circular fissure. The molten rock made its way through overlying sedimentary rocks. The fledgling volcano lacked the thrust necessary to reach the surface, however, and all the magma cooled off underground. Subsequent erosion and glaciation wore away much of the overlying bedrock, and exposed the igneous edge of the ring dike. The rocks at the border of the newly formed pluton (any body of igneous rock solidified far below the earth's surface) were metamorphosed by the extreme heat of the magma. This contact zone is clearly visible at the base of Crystal Cascade, where a second bedrock shows as a gray mass. Evidence of the ring dike formation can also be found at the top of the Cascades. Chunks of the surrounding bedrock were constantly consumed by the magma as it moved upwards. However, pieces that were only partially absorbed when the magma had cooled are said to be visible in the flat outcrops above the cliff. The only other large example of a ring dike is in Norway, where they call it a *nordmarkite*.

At 1.3 miles the trail levels slightly and you begin to see the Ascutney ridge line across the valley. After crossing the bottom of the valley and a brook, you climb a small bank and turn right on an old roadway. You are now on the old Weathersfield Trail, which is blazed in white, so expect a combination of white and blue blazes to the summit. Continue on the roadway past several rock outcrops to Halfway Brooks at 1.7 miles. Turn left and follow the sign's instructions to stay on the trail and not take shortcuts as you ascend the steep

ridge. Erosion in this area is a serious problem that you can help control by staying on the trail. Still climbing, you pass exposed rock outcrops where you can rest and enjoy the views. Swing right through some stunted birches and return to the woods on easier grades.

At 2.3 miles you make a sharp right turn to Gus's Lookout, a series of large rock outcrops with views of the valley and the summit ridge. The lookout was named for Augustus Aldrich, a hiker who died in 1974 on Mount Katahdin at age 86.

Return to the woods, pass a large boulder, and follow a switchback through a white birch, fern-filled grove. Bear left to a trail junction. A spur to the left leads to the west peak with views to the east of the Connecticut River Valley and to the west of the Green Mountain Range. Continue straight from the trail junction for nice views to the north. The summit, covered with antennas, is reached at 2.9 miles by taking a right at the junction and ascending through overgrowth. When leaving the summit, be careful *not* to take the white-blazed trail, which leads to a parking lot at the top of the Ascutney Toll Road.

Return to the junction and hike back down the trail to your car.

Central Vermont

23

Lincoln Gap

Total distance: 1.25 miles
Hiking time: 1 hour
Vertical rise: 600 feet
Rating: Easy to moderate
Map: USGS 7.5' Lincoln

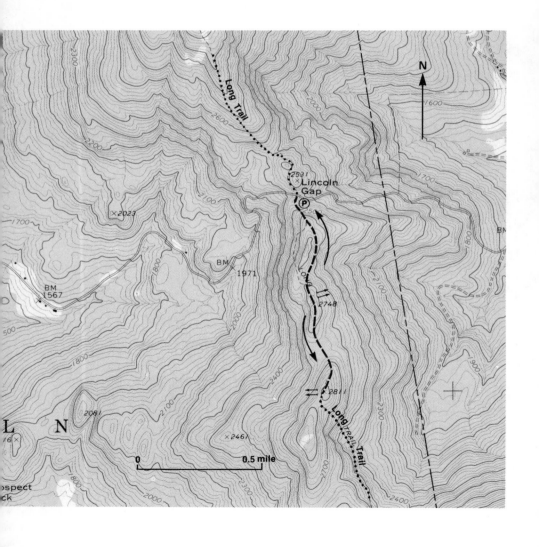

Lincoln Gap Overlook

This short hike, with excellent western views of the Green Mountain Range, passes through the Bread Loaf Wilderness, named after Bread Loaf Mountain, the highest point in the Wilderness. Established in 1984, the 21,480-acre wilderness includes seventeen miles of the Long Trail, eleven major peaks (all over 3,000 feet in elevation), and the Presidential Range (Mount Wilson, Mount Roosevelt, Mount Cleveland, and Mount Grant).

To reach the trail from the eastern side of the mountain, take VT 100 to Lincoln Gap Road (the sign says, "Lincoln Gap/Bristol") near Warren (0.0). Turn west off VT 100 on the Lincoln Gap Road. The road turns to dirt at 1.6 miles. At 2.8 miles the road is paved and ascends to the top of the gap at 4.3 miles.

From the western side of the mountain, drive east of Bristol (0.0) on VT 116/VT 17 to the turnoff to Lincoln and Lincoln Gap at 1.6 miles. Take this turnoff to the town of Lincoln at 5.1 miles. You reach a bridge and United States Forest Service Road 54 at 6.2 miles. At 7.5 miles the road turns to dirt. At 9.3 miles the road turns to pavement again and reaches the top of the gap at 9.9 miles.

Parking for eight cars is available just to the east of the gap summit. A new parking lot for fifteen to twenty more cars has been added to the east of the upper lot.

From the upper parking area, take the white-blazed Long Trail south from the gap. As you enter the woods, climb a small bank until you reach a Green Mountain National Forest registration box. A sign tells you that you are entering the Bread Loaf Wilderness. To the left is a steep ridge you will climb—but first begin a moderate ascent through yellow and white birches until you reach a double blaze and the first switchback. Turn left and begin a steep ascent. Partway up the ridge, rest and enjoy the view into the gap below. Notice metal signs on the trees which indicate the location of a benchmark—a surveyor's mark made on a permanent landmark of known position and altitude, and used as a reference point in determining other elevations.

Continue your ascent with limited views into the gap and of Mount Abraham to the north. Be sure to avoid all side trails in this section. Swing around the east ridge on a more gradual slope and begin a steep scramble over quite rocky terrain. The trail then follows along the ridge and opens up to good views east to Warren and the valley below, and north to Mount Abraham.

Continue your hike into the woods, across a wet area, and up another rocky section of trail. Notice the steeper slopes on both the west and east sides of the trail, as you ascend along a densely wooded ridge.

As the trail begins to descend slightly through softwoods, you step out onto Eastwoods Rise, an exposed rock face, at 0.6 mile. Enjoy the excellent views: west to Bristol and the Bristol Cliffs, south to Mount Grant, and north to Mount Abraham.

Hike back down the same way to your car, but be extremely careful as you descend the rocky sections of the trail. Even though it is a short trip, this hike is quite scenic, especially during fall foliage season.

24

Camel's Hump

Total distance: 7.4-mile loop
Hiking time: 6 hours
Vertical rise: 2,645 feet
Rating: Strenuous
Maps: USGS 7.5' Waterbury, Huntington

This difficult hike takes you to the 4,083-foot summit of Camel's Hump. The Waubanaukee Indians called Camel's Hump, "Tah-wak-be-dee-ee-wadso," which means "the saddle mountain." Legend says that Samuel de Champlain's explorers thought the mountain looked like a resting lion and called it "le lion couchant," or "the couching lion." In 1798, Ira Allen referred to the mountain as Camel's Rump on a historical map. From that name, Zadock Thompson called the mountain Camel's Hump in 1830.

During the Civil War, Camel's Hump was a well-known resort with horse and carriage trails leading to guest houses at the base and summit. Its popularity waned, however, with competition from the Mount Mansfield resort complex. In the early 1900s, area businessmen restored the trails and the summit house. Professor Will Monroe of the "Couching Lion Farm" (the trailhead of this hike) continued their efforts by developing a section of the Long Trail known as the "Monroe Skyline."

In 1911, Colonel Joseph Battell gave one thousand acres of land, including Camel's Hump, to the State of Vermont for one dollar. Colonel Battell specified

that the entire forest be "preserved in a primeval state." Through various purchases, exchanges, and gifts, the State had acquired approximately 7,478 acres by 1951.

The Department of Forests, Parks and Recreation defended a policy of limited building and regulated development on the Hump, until the summit and surrounding state land were declared a Natural Area in 1965. In 1968, the Hump was designated a Registered National Natural Landmark by the National Park Service. The Camel's Hump State Park, established by the Vermont Legislature in 1969, includes all lands extending from VT 17 north to the Winooski River and from the Huntington River to the Mad River. The Park now includes 19,474 acres of land.

Camel's Hump is one of the highest use areas in Vermont. Mostly used by day hikers, the mountain averages 10,000–15,000 hikers a year. Take time to observe the width of the trails and the extensive trailwork required by the heavy foot traffic. Such heavy use requires extensive and difficult trail maintenance, and constant attention to the protection of the summit's fragile arctic-alpine vegetation.

The survival of this rare vegetation, much of which looks like ordinary grass, is precarious. Shallow soils, vigorous climatic conditions, and slow-growing vegetation make the environment especially vulnerable to hiker disturbances. It takes approximately eighty years for a tree near the treeline to grow two inches in diameter.

When a small portion of alpine tundra is destroyed, the wind rapidly scours large holes in the damaged turf and the soil quickly erodes. Removal of rocks from the grassy tundra is especially

harmful in this respect. Fires destroy not only the ground cover plants, but the thin underlying layer of humus as well. Because excessive trampling of plants and soil leads to further loss of rare vegetation, hikers should stay on the marked trails and rock outcrops. Green Mountain Club/State Ranger-Naturalists, on duty during the hiking season, assist hikers and explain the fragile nature of this environment. Be sure to follow their instructions.

To reach the trail, begin at the junction of US 2 and VT 100 (0.0 miles) in Waterbury. Take US 2 east 0.2 mile and turn right (south) on Winooski Street. Cross the iron bridge over the river at 0.4 mile and turn right. At 4.6 miles turn left (south) onto Camel's Hump Road. There are several side roads off the Hump Road, so be careful to stay on the main road. At 6.0 miles bear left at the fork and cross the bridge. At 8.3 miles, parking for twenty to twenty-five cars is available at the Couching Lion Farm parking lot at the end of the road. Parking may also be available in an additional lot which was under construction in 1989.

Follow the blue-blazed trail from the parking area into the woods, and come to a trail register and information board. Because you will be following several trails throughout this loop hike, take time to review the information board and trail map before beginning your hike. From the register box you follow the blue-blazed Forestry and Dean Trails.

After crossing a brook, pass by old stone walls and an overgrown pasture. Cross another brook at 0.8 mile, and climb to a trail junction at 1.3 miles. To the right is the Forestry Trail on which you will return. Turn left along the Dean Trail. At 1.5 miles you cross Camel's Hump Brook and soon pass the Hump Brook Testing Area. Continue uphill,

cross a birch-covered knob at 2.0 miles, and reach an area of beaver activity. Enjoy the view over the beaver pond to Camel's Hump.

Beyond the pond, the Dean Trail ascends through a notch to the Long Trail junction. The trail ahead leads 0.2 mile to Montclair Glen Lodge, a frame cabin with bunks for twelve, built in 1948 by the Long Trail Patrol. During the hiking season a Green Mountain Club Caretaker is in residence and a small fee is charged for overnight use. A sharp left turn takes you to the Long Trail south via the Allis Trail.

Turn right (north) on the white-blazed Long Trail and steeply ascend past the rock face you saw from the beaver pond. At the top of the rock face, there is a nice view of the pond and valley below, as well as Mount Ethan Allen to the south. The trail climbs along the rock outcrop, enters a cleft in the rock at 2.6 miles, and reaches an overlook. Ascend another knob, and enjoy the view ahead of the rocky Camel's Hump summit.

Next, descend toward the west side of the ridge, drop into a col with occasional views, and ascend again at 3.4 miles. There are several views of the summit as you steeply traverse the southwest face of the mountain. At 3.8 miles you reach the Alpine Trail junction. This yellow-blazed trail can be used to bypass the summit in bad weather. Continue north on the Long Trail, hike up the exposed western face of the Hump, and reach the 4,083-foot summit at 4.0 miles. Remember the fragile nature of this summit area and be sure to stay on the marked trails and rock outcrops. Help to protect this endangered ecosystem.

On a clear day there are spectacular views from the summit. To the south are Mounts Ethan and Ira Allen, Lincoln

Camel's Hump from the trail

Ridge with wide ski trails, and Killington and Pico peaks. To the north are Mount Mansfield, Belvidere Mountain, with the white scar of the asbestos mine, and Owl's Head in Canada. To the east are the Worcester and Granite Mountains, and the White Mountains of New Hampshire, including Mount Washington and the Presidential Range, as well as Mount Moosilauke and the Franconia Range. To the west are the Champlain Valley and New York's Adirondack Mountains, with Whiteface Mountain standing alone to the north.

After you rest and enjoy the scenery, continue north on the Long Trail. The descent is steep on the rocky trail to the Hut Clearing and the Forestry Trail junc-

tion on the right at 4.3 miles. The sign indicates a distance of 3.1 miles back to your car. Take the blue-blazed Forestry Trail, at first steeply and then more moderately downhill, until you reach the yellow-blazed Alpine Trail at 4.9 miles. Continue to descend the Forestry Trail through mixed hard and softwoods. You cross Camel's Hump Brook at 5.2 miles and soon walk along the base of a large rockface. At 5.4 miles you descend a birch ridge, then hike over rocks which have fallen from the outcrop above you. At 6.1 miles you reach the Forestry/Dean Trail junction and complete your loop. Continue back downhill to the parking area at 7.4 miles.

Mount Moosalamoo

Total distance: 4.8 miles
Hiking time: 3 hours
Vertical rise: 1,320 feet
Rating: Moderate
Map: GMNF 7.5′ East Middlebury

Mount Moosalamoo summit

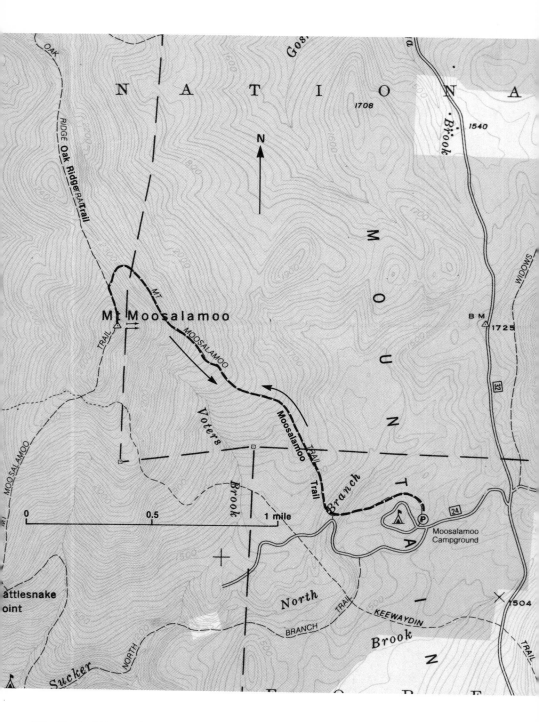

This trail, constructed in 1975 by the Youth Conservation Corps, offers a pleasant mountain hike and ridge walk, a nice view from an overlook near the wooded summit, and fewer hikers.

To reach the trail, drive 10.8 miles west of Hancock, or 0.9 mile east of Ripton, on VT 125 to United States Forest Service (USFS) Road-FR 32 (0.0). Turn south on FR 32 and drive 3.3 miles to FR 24, which is marked by a sign to the Moosalamoo Campground and Voter Brook Overlook. Drive west on FR 24 to the campground at 3.8 miles. Just before you enter the campground road loop, there is a twenty-car parking lot for hikers on the right. The blue-blazed trail starts from the parking lot and is marked by a USFS sign indicating a distance of 2.4 miles to the summit.

Begin your hike by climbing over a small knoll and descending through young hardwoods. There are occasional views of the ridge across the valley. Cross an old road and steeply descend to cross the north branch of Voter Brook on a bridge at 0.5 mile. The trail crosses a wet area on puncheon, then ascends and becomes drier. Puncheon are small wooden bridges of one or more logs or board planks held off the ground on sills. Enjoy the ferns along the trail, as you climb on easy grades. Cross another wet area and continue to climb through mixed hardwoods. Hobblebush and nettles appear as you hike among boulders up the hillside at 1.0 mile. The dense forest can confuse your sense of direction, but the path of the trail is obvious.

At 1.4 miles you reach a rock outcrop where you can take a break and enjoy a nice rest. The trail takes a sharp left on a switchback and climbs onto a ridge. As the trail levels, you get a view of another ridge ahead. The numerous old logging roads in this area are evidence of former logging activity. Blazes are faint, but the trail is still easy to follow. You pass by several large boulders and cross an old road.

At 2.1 miles make a sharp left and climb steeply along switchbacks to the junction of the Oak Ridge Trail. Turn left (south) on this trail and climb the occasionally steep, hardwood ridgeline to a northeastern viewpoint on the left of the valley below you. Continue along the ridge to the wooded 2,620-foot summit.

Hike back down the same trail to your car.

26

Worth Mountain

Total distance: 6 miles
Hiking time: 4 hours
Vertical rise: 1,735 feet
Rating: Moderate
Map: USGS 7.5' Bread Loaf

Worth Mountain, just south of the Middlebury Gap and Snow Bowl, has a 3,234-foot summit covered in dense softwoods and excellent views to the north and south at two overlooks. This is a trail of contrasts: from an old overgrown logging road with nettle patches to a softwood ridge with nice views.

To reach the trail, drive 8.2 miles west of Hancock, or 3.6 miles east of Ripton, on VT 125 to United States Forest Service (USFS) Road-FR 67 (0.0). Turn south on FR 67. Avoid a spur to the right at 0.2 mile and stay on the main road. At 1.4 mile the road forks and you go right. The left fork is gated. At 4.1 miles you reach the end of the road and a parking area for five to six cars.

From the parking area, a USFS sign states that this area is used for primitive camping and indicates a distance of 1.0 mile to the Long Trail junction. Begin your hike on the blue-blazed Sucker Brook Trail. Make a sharp left at an old log landing just beyond the sign and follow a grassy old logging road. You soon pass a USFS register box. Raspberry bushes provide seasonal snacks and there is a view on your left of the ridge ahead. Because the road is quite overgrown, this portion of the trail is not impressive. However, the summit views are worth the effort.

At 0.3 mile the trail branches right and enters the woods. You cross numerous old logging roads and nettle patches, until you reach the Long Trail junction at 1.0 mile. Turn left and follow the white-blazed Long Trail north. Cross a brook and reach Sucker Brook Shelter, which was built by the USFS in 1963 and provides overnight space for six to eight hikers.

Continue north from the shelter on the Long Trail and ascend over a wet nettle area on wood and stone steps. You quickly cross a gully above the shelter and see evidence of past logging activity. Ascend through birches, and pass over and through numerous nettle patches. Look for occasional views of the ridge ahead. At 2.0 miles descend to a low spot, and then begin the final climb up a pleasant, birch-lined ridge. At 2.4 miles you reach a lookout, and then climb some log stairs onto the dense spruce and fir-covered ridgeline. In contrast to the ascent thus far, the trail levels a little and reaches the wooded summit of Worth Mountain at

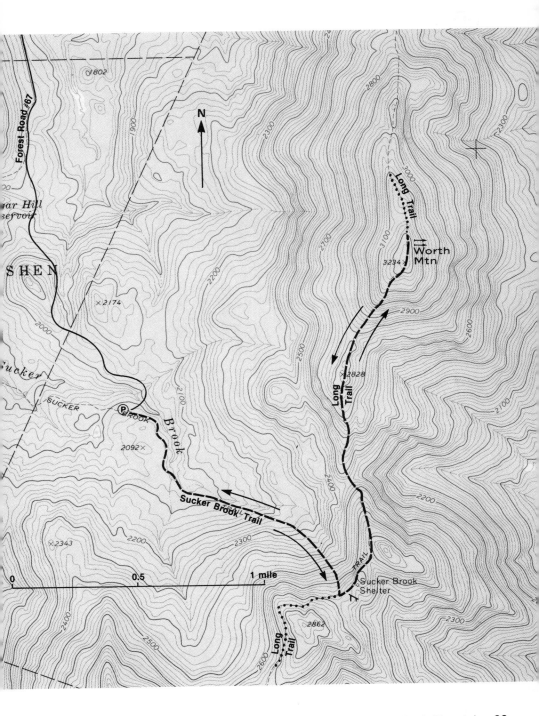

Forest Road #67

1802

N

SHEN

SUCKER

P

BROOK

Sucker

Brook

Brook

×2174

2092×

×2343

Sucker Brook Trail

0   0.5   1 mile

Sucker Brook Shelter

TRAIL

Long Trail

2862

Long Trail

Worth Mtn

3234×

×2828

Long Trail

Trail up Worth Mountain

2.9 miles. Continue downhill north of the summit to the east lookout at 3.0 miles. From the rock outcrop enjoy a beautiful eastern view of Monastery Mountain.

Hike back down the same trails to the parking area.

27

Mount Abraham

Total distance: 5.2 miles
Hiking time: 5 hours
Vertical rise: 2,500 feet
Rating: Strenuous
Map: USGS 7.5' Lincoln

The spectacular views from the 4,006-foot summit of Mount Abraham make this hike one of the most popular in Vermont. On a clear day, you can see the Adirondack Mountains in New York, the White Mountains in New Hampshire, and the Green Mountain Range from Killington Peak to Belvidere Mountain.

To reach the trailhead, start in the town of Lincoln. At a rock memorial marker in the center of town (0.0), take a left (north) on Quaker Street. Pass the Town Clerk's office on the right. At 0.7 mile turn right (east) on United States Forest Service (USFS) Road-FR 350 and proceed up a long hill. At 2.0 miles you reach a fork where you bear right, still on FR 350. The road becomes much narrower. Stay left on FR 350 at another fork. Continue to the parking area on the left for six cars at 3.2 miles.

Across from the parking area, begin your hike at the trailhead sign which indicates a distance of two miles to the Long Trail and Battell Shelter. Enter the woods on the blue-blazed Battell Trail, and quickly reach a trail register. Swing left and ascend up a moss-covered hill. The trail then levels and you enter a sugarbush.

Over the years, Vermont sugar makers have produced more maple syrup per year than any other maple producing state. Depending on spring weather, they produce up to 500,000 gallons of maple syrup each year. Approximately forty gallons of maple sap, collected in the sugar lines you pass, produce just one gallon of pure maple syrup. Vermont maple syrup is required to have a heavier density than U.S. standards and to be free of preservatives. Look for the term "Vermont Maple Syrup," if you decide to take some home with you.

After you pass under and along several sugar lines, cross a wet area on flat rocks and ascend some steep switchbacks. Portions of the upper sugar lines can be seen off the trail. At 0.7 mile the trail bears right and ascends to a brook crossing. The trail soon becomes rocky and turns left on an old road at 1.2 mile. (Note this junction for your return hike.) The wide road continues uphill on a steep grade over long switchbacks and enters some softwoods. The road, less defined because of erosion, may be wet in places. Cross a small brook at 1.8 miles, and then leave the road for only a

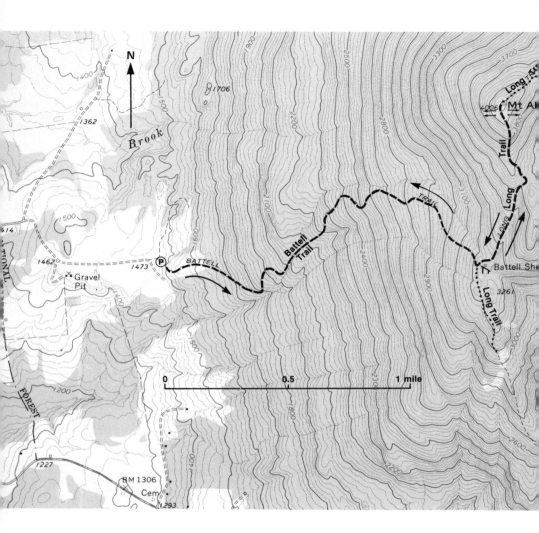

short distance. Ascend the rocky, eroded road to the Long Trail junction at 2.0 miles.

Hike straight uphill on the Long Trail to Battell Shelter. The trail in this section, quite wide and on easy grades, follows an old carriage road built in the late 1800s by Joseph Battell, proprietor of the Breadloaf Inn. The Battell Shelter was constructed in 1967 by campers from Farm and Wilderness Camps using materials airlifted to the site by helicopter. The shelter has bunk space for six to eight hikers and is maintained by the Green Mountain Club and the United States Forest Service.

Continue uphill on the Long Trail along the very rocky, old carriage road, with occasional views of the summit ahead. At 2.3 miles leave the roadway and hike up steep grades, often on exposed bedrock scars. Look south and enjoy views back to the trail you just climbed. Next, scramble up an exposed rock face, and return briefly to smaller softwoods before you begin your final ascent to the summit.

The trees are now waist high as you ascend to the open rock summit at 2.9 miles. Two small rock walls provide shelter from the winds, as you enjoy one of the best panoramic views in Vermont. To the east are the White Mountains; to the west, the Bristol Cliffs, Lake Champlain and the Adirondack Mountains; and to the south and north are the Green Mountains—from Killington Peak to Belvidere Mountain.

The summit supports a community of small, rare, arctic-alpine plants—the patches of "grass" and soil among the summit rocks. While on the summit, avoid disturbing any of these endangered plants by hiking only on the trail and rocks.

Hike back down the trails to your car.

Mount Grant

Total distance: 8.4 miles
Hiking time: 5 hours
Vertical rise: 1,960 feet
Rating: Strenuous
Map: USGS 7.5' Lincoln

The scenic Cooley Glen trail up Mount Grant follows old logging roads along the New Haven River. Though overgrown in places, the logging roads are dry and follow gradual grades, except for very steep sections near the top of the trail. Several swimming holes in the river provide the opportunity for a refreshing summer splash after (or maybe even before) your long hike.

Take the Lincoln-Warren Highway, 1.0 mile east of Lincoln, or 3.7 miles west of the Lincoln Gap summit, to the road crossing of the New Haven River. Turn south on United States Forest Service (USFS) Road-FR 57 (0.0) and drive 4.2 miles through South Lincoln and along the river to the junction of FR 201. There is a trail sign at this junction which lists the Cooley Glen and Emily Proctor trails. Turn east on FR 201. Drive to and park at a USFS "dispersed camping site" at 4.6 miles.

At the trailhead register, note the Emily Proctor Trail, which turns right. Instead, take the blue-blazed Cooley Glen Trail, which follows the gravel road along the New Haven River. Cross the river on a bridge at 0.3 mile and reach a clearing, once an old log landing. The trail leaves the far end of the clearing at a deep ditch and follows the river on almost level grades over a wide, overgrown, old logging road. You soon see a road junction, as the trail bears right and parallels the river. At 1.0 mile you cross several deep waterbars and tributaries, as you move away from, and then return to, the river. No blazes are visible along this portion of the trail, except for occasional blue-blazed rocks in the grassy road.

Waterbars, a drainage system of log or rock construction, are the best defense against trail erosion. A waterbar is composed of three parts: the bar built of log or rock; the apron, a shallow slope to funnel water to the bar and ditch; and the ditch to carry water off the trail.

At 1.5 miles the road becomes quite wet and rocky. Enter the woods to avoid this wet area, and then return to cross a tributary near the remains of an old bridge. This point marks the entrance to the Bread Loaf Wilderness, which was named for 3,835-foot Bread Loaf mountain. Established in 1984, the 21,480 acre Wilderness includes seventeen miles of the Long Trail, eleven major peaks (all over 3,000 feet in elevation),

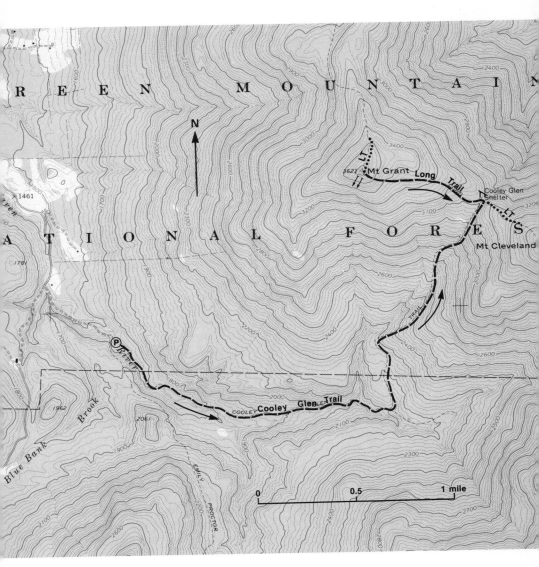

and the Presidential Range (Mount Wilson, Mount Roosevelt, Mount Cleveland, and Mount Grant).

Continue your hike, moving away from the river, ascend slightly, and swing left along the old road. Blue blazes can be seen on the trees. At 1.9 miles you climb until you pass through a scenic, more mature forest. At 2.5 miles the trail levels after a short ascent and you can see Mount Grant through the trees on your left. The trail ascends steeply along a gully, passes through a rocky nettle patch, then crosses the small brook you

View along Mount Grant Trail

could hear during your climb up the gully. Begin a long hike uphill, cross a small brook, pass a spur trail, and reach the junction of the Long Trail at 3.3 miles.

Turn left and follow the white-blazed Long Trail north several yards to Cooley Glen Shelter. Take time for a well-deserved rest. The shelter, built by the United States Forest Service in 1965, is a frame lean-to with bunk space for six to eight hikers.

Beyond the shelter, continue north on the Long Trail. The hike to Mount Grant's summit is easy compared to the trail you just climbed. Look for southern views before the trail swings right and you ascend again. By 4.0 miles the mixed forest turns to predominantly spruce. The trees become more stunted as you hike along switchbacks to the southern overlook. Just beyond is the 3,623-foot wooded summit of Mount Grant at 4.2 miles. From the southern overlook you can see the New Haven River basin, Mount Cleveland, Mount Roosevelt, Mount Wilson, and Bread Loaf Mountain.

Hike back down the same trails to the parking area at the campsite.

Mount Independence

Total distance: 2.5 miles
Hiking time: 2 hours
Vertical rise: 200 feet
Rating: Easy to moderate
Map: USGS 15' Ticonderoga

Mount Independence, often called the "most interesting and important historic site in Vermont," was Vermont's major Revolutionary fortification and is one of the least disturbed Revolutionary sites in the United States. The Mount's stone chert outcroppings and the area's abundant food resources attracted Native Americans thousands of years before European discovery. Mount Independence is protected on three sides by water and steep cliffs and is accessible only from the south. This protection, plus its 200-foot elevation above the lake, made the Mount an important component of America's defense against a British attack from Canada during the war.

The northern half of Mount Independence was purchased in 1912 by Sarah Pell, who worked to preserve the site. In 1952–53 her son John, who had inherited the land, deeded the property to the Fort Ticonderoga Association, "an educational institution chartered explicitly to ensure the conservation, interpretation, and preservation of Fort Ticonderoga and neighboring sites." In 1961 and 1973 the State of Vermont purchased over 108 acres to enhance the Association's effort.

Mount Independence is open from Memorial Day to Columbus Day, Wednesday through Sunday from 9:30 AM to 5:30 PM. A caretaker is available to give guided tours of the site upon request. There are grazing animals on the site which should not be disturbed. Because the area is an important archaeological site held in public trust, digging, metal detecting, and artifact collecting are against the law.

1989 marked the first phase in the development of a historic interpretation at Mount Independence as part of the Heritage '91 plan. Heritage '91, approved by the State Legislature in 1988, is a ten year management plan for developing and improving state-owned historic sites in celebration of the state bicentennial. After several seasons of archaeological investigation at Mount Independence, a Visitor's Center will be built to house exhibits.

To reach Mount Independence take VT 22A to the intersection of VT 73 (0.0), west of Orwell. Turn west on VT 73. At 0.3 mile bear left off VT 73 at a road junction, and avoid a side road on the left, as the road swings right. At 4.8 miles the paved road turns to gravel. At 5.2 miles you reach the Catfish Bay

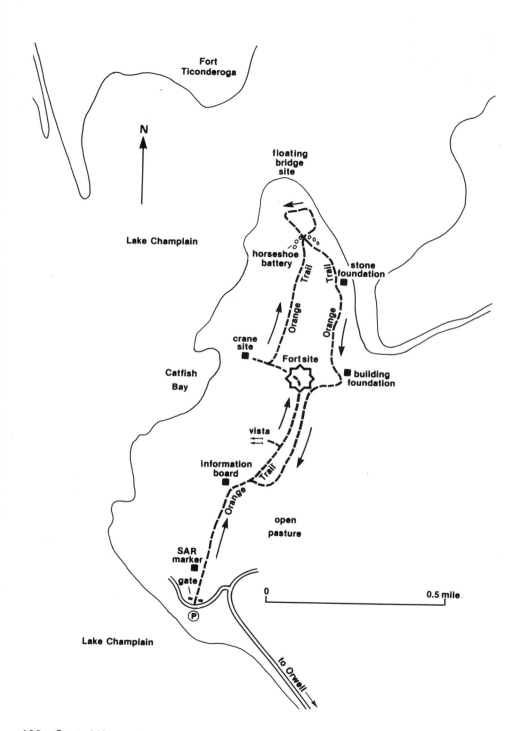

Fort
Ticonderoga

N

floating
bridge
site

Lake Champlain

horseshoe
battery

stone
foundation

Orange Trail

Orange Trail

crane
site

Fort site

building
foundation

Catfish
Bay

vista

information
board

Orange Trail

open
pasture

SAR
marker

gate

0   0.5 mile

P

Lake Champlain

to Orwell

Road junction. Turn left and drive up the steep narrow road. At 5.3 miles park in the lot at the top of the hill on the left side of the road in a meadow.

Begin your hike at the gate across the road from the parking lot. Bear left and go into a small wooded area, where there is a bronze plaque imbedded in a "sentry rock" by the Sons of the America Revolution. The plaque provides historical information about Mount Independence.

Return to the gate and continue to the top of the pasture where there is an information board with trail descriptions and area maps. Although four trails lead to the mountain, this description covers the Orange Trail, which takes you 2.5 miles past several interesting historical sites.

From the information post the Orange Trail bears north, but quickly branches to the left (west) of the White Trail. You soon pass over the top of the mountain and reach an overlook of Lake Champlain and Mount Defiance. Continue between woods and pasture on easy grades to a clearing where you bear left at 0.5 mile. Logs have been placed on the ground to indicate the layout of the Star Fort, the central stronghold on Mount Independence. The square parade ground is marked by cedars which have grown up along the lines of the barrack walls. Just ahead is an old well believed to have originated in the Revolutionary War period.

At 0.6 mile you reach a spur trail to the site of a huge crane used to hoist cannon, equipment, and supplies up to

the fort from ships anchored below in Catfish Bay. Continue your hike through the woods to a clearing, at 0.8 mile, that was the site of shops for blacksmiths, armorers, rope makers, wheelwrights, and other skilled craftsmen. Return to the woods, where you soon see a monument in the middle of a horseshoe-shaped battery. Here, cannon once commanded Lake Champlain to the north and the narrows between Mount Independence and Fort Ticonderoga. Next, descend to a shore battery that once guarded the vulnerable north shore of Lake Champlain. Continue your descent to the shoreline and the former site of a floating bridge which connected Mount Independence and Fort Ticonderoga. The bridge was twelve feet wide and anchored to twenty-two sunken piers. The trail follows the shoreline to an outcrop above the lake where ships are believed to have been masted.

Next, leave the shoreline, return to the horseshoe battery, and bear left to complete your loop. As you pass through a wooded area at 1.7 miles, look for the foundation of a possible observation shelter and another old rectangular foundation. You again cross logs at 2.0 miles which indicate the outline of the fort. Hike through the pasture, and return to the information board at 2.5 miles.

The Orange Trail is typical of the other three trails on Mount Independence. If you have time, consider exploring the other sites.

30

Skylight Pond

Total distance: 4.6 mile loop
Hiking time: 4–5 hours
Vertical rise: 1,620 feet
Rating: Moderately strenuous
Map: USGS 7.5' Bread Loaf

Skylight Pond is a high elevation pond located on the Long Trail, between Battell and Bread Loaf Mountains. Moose have occasionally been sighted at this shallow pond, and the sundew, a carnivorous bog plant, lives along the pond's shore.

To reach the trail, drive 2.8 miles east of Ripton or 9.0 miles west of VT 100 on VT 125 to United States Forest Service (USFS) Road-FR 59. Follow FR 59 north to Stream Mill Clearing on the right side of the road at 3.6 miles. Parking for ten to fifteen cars is provided at the clearing.

From the parking area, the blue-blazed trail enters the woods along an old logging road parallel to a brook. You soon reach a registration box where you should sign in, both for safety reasons and to provide trail-use data to help trail maintenance and protection programs.

The trail bears right at a fork, and crosses the brook on puncheon, a bridge of one or more logs or board planks held off the ground on sills. You then enter an area of former logging activity, now overgrown with yellow birch, beech, and maple trees. Numerous old logging roads intersect the trail, so be careful to follow the blazes. Crisscross the brook and start to ascend at 0.4 mile. Deep waterbars help stop trail erosion, as well as discourage vehicles from using the old roadway. You soon reach a signpost that indicates that you are entering the Breadloaf Wilderness, which was named for Bread Loaf Mountain, the highest point in the Wilderness, at 3,835 feet. Established in 1984, the 21,480-acre Wilderness includes seventeen miles of the Long Trail, eleven major peaks (all over 3,000 feet in elevation), and the Presidential Range (Mount Wilson, Mount Roosevelt, Mount Cleveland, and Mount Grant).

As the trail ascends, you cross the brook twice. There are limited views of the Bread Loaf Mountain ridgeline along this section of the trail. Continue through a wet area on an old overgrown road, cross the brook, bear right, and follow along the brook. Cross the brook again and swing right, go back onto the road, then take a sharp right off the road. At 0.7 mile you cross a wet area, as the trail winds uphill along a series of switchbacks.

At 1.1 miles you have limited views of Bread Loaf Mountain to the north. Follow a brook gully toward a notch in the

Skyline Lodge at Skylight Pond

ridgeline, through a forest of yellow birch, spruce, and hemlock. You soon start a steeper climb around a small spruce and balsam knob. You can see the summit ahead after cresting the knob at 1.6 miles. The ridge opens up into a sunny path, but you soon return to the denser softwoods and ascend again.

Enjoy the views to the west, as you begin a steep climb through several large boulders to the actual ridgeline. Continue uphill to the Long Trail junction, where the sign indicates a distance of two miles back to your car. The shelter is on the side trail straight ahead, but first turn right and follow the Long Trail to an unmarked side trail on the right. This spur trail leads to a great western overlook, at 2.1 miles, of Lake Champlain and the Adirondack Mountains. Return to the junction and take the side trail down to Skyline Lodge and Skylight Pond at 2.4 miles.

A new cedar log shelter, Skyline Lodge was built in 1987 by the United States Forest Service and the Green Mountain Club to replace the old shelter, which had deteriorated and become unsafe. Several thousand pounds of twenty-foot cedar logs, cement, and other materials were airlifted to the site by the Vermont Air National Guard. Now one of the nicest shelters on the Long Trail, the lodge looks out over beautiful Skylight Pond.

After resting at the shelter, return to the junction at 2.6 miles and hike down the trail to your car.

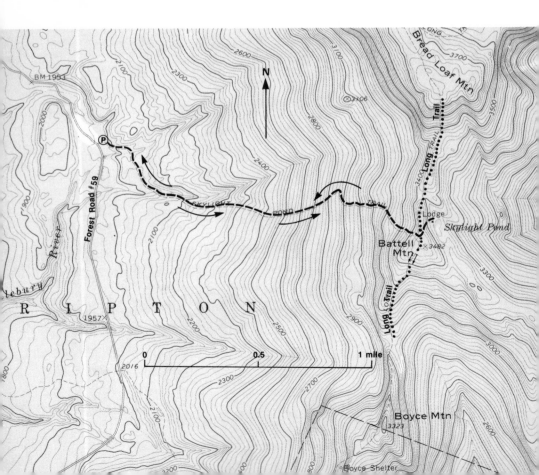

31

Burnt Rock Mountain

Total distance: 6.2-mile loop
Hiking time: 5 hours
Vertical rise: 2,020 feet
Rating: Strenuous
*Map: USGS 7.5' Waterbury, Mount Ellen, Waitsfield,
  Huntington*

This difficult but interesting hike follows the Hedgehog Brook Trail to the summit of Burnt Rock Mountain which, despite its relatively low 3,168-foot elevation, is treeless and offers excellent views of several neighboring mountains.

To reach the trail, drive north on VT 100 from Waitsfield (0.0) to the North Fayston Road at 5.0 miles. Turn left (west) on the North Fayston Road. At 7.5 miles the road turns to dirt. Continue to a fork at 9.2 miles. Go straight ahead. The road soon becomes one lane. You reach a gate and small five car parking area at 10.2 miles. This trail is on private property and only open to the public through the generosity and cooperation of the Big Basin Land Association. Please respect their wishes and park only at the parking area before the gate. Do not block the road or drive through the gate, and needless to say do not go near or enter the cabins—please stay on the trail!

Be attentive at the beginning of this hike. The trail follows the gravel road past the camps and may be somewhat confusing, as there are no blazes until you enter the woods.

From the parking area, walk through the gate and follow the gravel road parallel to the brook until you reach a road junction and a camp. Go straight across the bridge and past another camp on the left. Turn left, cross a small bridge, turn right just before the camp, and enter the woods. The trail is somewhat overgrown along the brook.

An old logging road enters from the left, as you begin to climb a rolling hill. Cross two brooks, hike uphill through an occasional nettle patch, and enter some young hardwoods. Cross another brook at 1.0 mile before continuing uphill through a valley.

At 1.4 miles the trail swings left and follows a ridge onto a plateau. Large boulders appear as you ascend the hillside. Enjoy occasional views of the Waitsfield valley.

You reach another plateau and a brook at 2.0 miles. At this point, *ignore a double-blaze and go straight* through a slightly wet area to stay on the trail. Pass through another valley and begin a steep climb along several switchbacks. Be careful as you negotiate roots and scramble over rocks. The trail soon makes a sharp left, then a sharp right, and at 2.5 miles reaches the Long Trail.

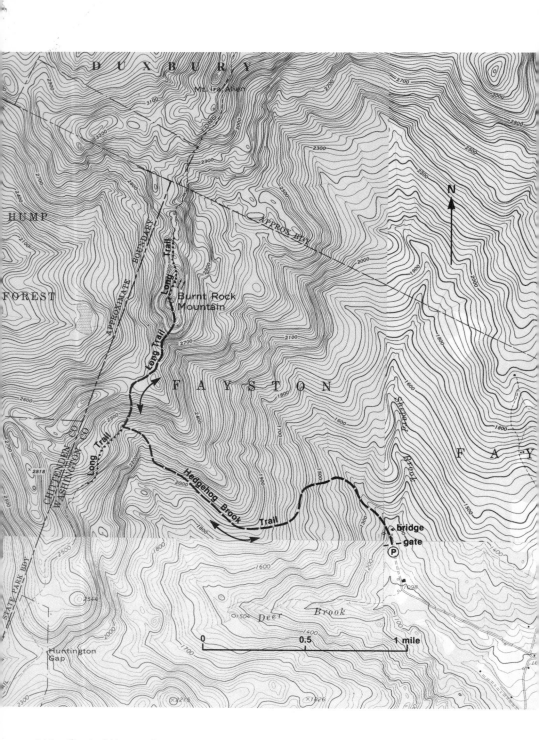

Burnt Rocks

A left would take you south on the the Long Trail to Cowles Cove Shelter, but you turn right and hike north.

Continue on the Long Trail along the ridgeline, with several views of Burnt Rock Mountain. You climb through a moss-covered rocky area and a cleft in the rocks, and begin an even steeper climb, until you work your way along a large rock wall. The white blazes on the wall are outlined with red to aid in poor visibility. You squeeze through cracks in the rocks, skirt a cliff, and ascend a gully on the west side of a large rock outcrop.

Hike up the open ridge to the 3,168-foot summit at 3.1 miles. To the north are views of Mounts Ira and Ethan Allen, and Camel's Hump; to the west, Lake Champlain; to the east, the Northfield Range and the Granite Mountains; and to the south, Lincoln Ridge. After enjoying a well-deserved rest and the views, hike back down the trail to your car.

Deer Leap Mountain

Total distance: 2.5-mile loop
Hiking time: 3 hours
Vertical rise: 570 feet
Rating: Moderate with very difficult descent
Map: USGS 7.5' Pico Peak

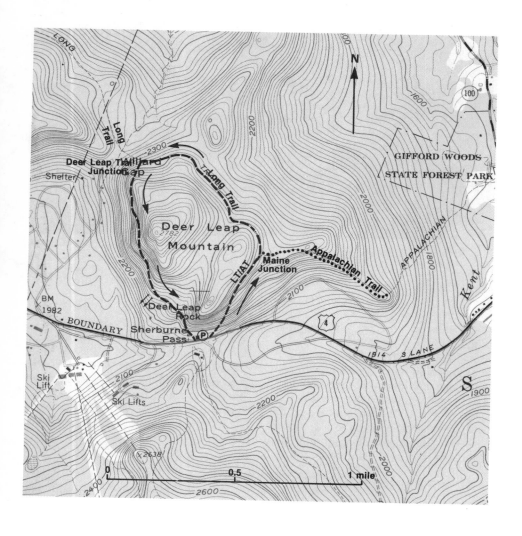

Deer Leap with Pico Peak in the background

The Deer Leap Trail is a unique loop hike that includes portions of the Long and Appalachian trails, and a side trail that completes the loop by going over Deer Leap Cliffs and descending to Sherburne Pass. The cliffs are a popular climbing area, so be sure to look for rock climbers.

In southern Vermont, the Long and Appalachian trails coincide from the Massachusetts border to "Maine Junc-tion." The Long Trail continues north to Canada, while the Appalachian Trail goes east through Vermont, across the White Mountains in New Hampshire, to Maine. Built by volunteers between 1921 and 1937, the Appalachian Trail extends 2,100 miles from Springer Mountain in Georgia to Mount Katahdin in Maine. The Appalachian Trail was first proposed in 1921 by Benton MacKaye, a forester, author, and philosopher. On

Stratton Mountain in Vermont, MacKaye conceived of the idea to connect the high peaks of the East, after construction of the Long Trail had already begun. Today, over eighty local, state, and federal agencies; the Appalachian Trail Conference; local non-profit trail groups like the Green Mountain Club; individual volunteers; community groups; and over a thousand private landowners—in fourteen states—work together to maintain and preserve this valuable recreational resource.

To reach the trail, take US 4 to the top of Sherburne Pass (about 9 miles east of Rutland) and the Inn at Long Trail. The Inn offers parking for eight cars (no overnight parking allowed). There is also space for twenty-five cars on the south side of US 4.

Begin your hike on the north side of US 4 and follow the white-blazed Long Trail/Appalachian Trail over the first set of boulders, past the blue-blazed trail on the left. You will return on this trail. You soon pass through a boulder field, hike up some steps, and cross the face of a large rock outcrop. At 0.5 mile you reach Maine Junction, where the white-blazed Appalachian Trail branches right. You continue straight ahead, north on the white-blazed Long Trail, through a hardwood forest and nettles, and over rolling ground along rock slabs. At 1.2 miles you reach the junction of the northern end of the blue-blazed Deer Leap Trail. This marked junction is the halfway point in your hike.

Turn left at the junction, start a gradual ascent, and climb steeply until you pass over a spruce knob. Avoid the unblazed spur trails that appear to lead to lookouts—they don't! Listen for traffic from US 4 and enjoy views of Pico Peak. At 1.9 miles you see a sign for "Deer Leap Height" and directions to US 4 and the Long Trail junction.

Begin a steep descent just beyond the sign, cross a small brook, and hike through a dip between two hills. Ascend through birches and climb straight up a large rock outcrop. Because the trail may be brushy, be careful not to drop off the crest of the hill. Bear right to a rock outcrop over which you lower yourself. At 2.3 miles walk out onto the upper lookout.

Enjoy views of Pico Peak directly across from you, Sherburne Pass below you, and sweeping views to the east, south, and west. Return to the main trail located near the ledge before the overlook. It descends through the woods, avoiding the steep rock overlook, and then passes beneath it. Due to erosion, the descent to Route 4 can be best described as an extremely steep rock scramble; be careful as you pick your route down the hillside. Hikers unsure of their rock-scrambling ability may prefer to hike the trail in the reverse direction, climbing this slope at the outset, or avoid this popular day trip altogether.

Northern Vermont

Black Creek and Maquam Creek Trails
Missisquoi National Wildlife Refuge

Total distance: 2.7 miles
Hiking time: 1–2 hours
Vertical rise: 25 feet
Rating: Easy
Map: USGS 7.5' East Alburg

These self-guided nature trails are in the 5,651-acre Missisquoi National Wildlife Refuge, which occupies much of the Missisquoi River delta and consists of marsh, open water, and wooded swamp. "Missisquoi," an Abnaki word, means an area of "much waterfowl" and "much grass." The refuge was established in 1942 to provide feeding, nesting, and resting areas for migrating waterfowl. During the peak of the fall migration there may be as many as 22,000 ducks present on the refuge at one time. The largest concentrations of waterfowl occur during April, September, and October. A variety of other birds are also present during spring, summer, and fall, including great horned owls, barred owls, ospreys, and an occasional bald eagle.

Remember to bring binoculars, and walk slowly and quietly so you do not disturb the birds and wildlife. Time needed to hike this 1.5-mile loop will vary depending on how long you stop to observe your surroundings.

From Swanton (0.0), drive 2.4 miles west on VT 78 to the National Wildlife Refuge headquarters on the left side of the road. Parking is located behind the office. A large information board with a map of the refuge is located at the back of the parking area. A box at the board includes a trail map for the "Black Creek and Maquam Creek Trails," as well as other information pamphlets. Some of the signposts which line the nature trail are in disrepair and may be missing. Note that the information pamphlet's 1.5 mile trail distance does not include walking in and out on the mowed roadway.

The trail starts at the information board and crosses the large meadow and railroad tracks into a wooded area. On a clear day, you immediately begin to hear birds as you follow the trail along the wide, mowed roadway and across the railroad tracks. Through the brush on the left, look for a very black meandering creek and possibly some beaver activity. Also, watch for game trails, which crisscross this section of the trail. On the right, you soon see the remnants of an old, now overgrown goose pen, constructed in the 1950s to establish a resident breeding flock of Canada geese.

At 0.3 mile another mowed roadway, the Maquam Creek Trail, enters from the right. You will return by this trail. Con-

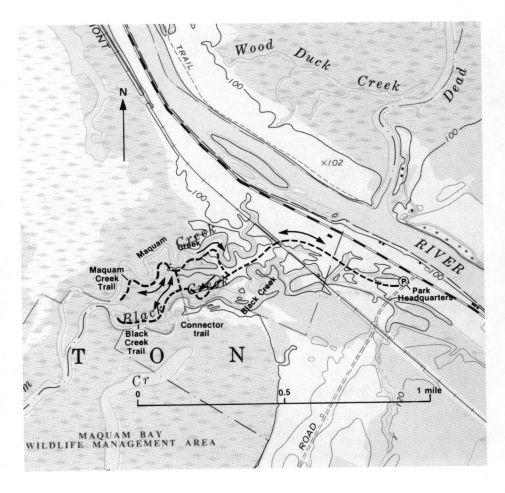

tinue straight ahead to the end of the mowed roadway and the beginning of the Black Creek Trail, which follows the bank of the Black Creek. Black and slow moving, the creek lives up to its name. Take time to observe the reflections of the white birches, as they make a nice contrast in the black water. Enjoy your time, but be prepared for a few (maybe many!) mosquitos during bug season. Look for the remnants of an old camp along the opposite bank.

At 0.6 mile you reach a trail junction where a sign indicates a distance of 0.2 mile to the end of the Black Creek Trail. Follow along the Black Creek bank to the end of the trail. Turn around and return to the junction at 1.0 mile.

From the junction, take the connector trail to the Maquam Creek Trail at 1.1 miles. A sign indicates 0.5 mile to the end of this trail. Turn left and hike parallel to Maquam Creek. Look for lots of ducks along the creek, as well as nesting boxes. The trail may be wet and/or flooded at times.

Missisquoi

At 1.6 miles you reach Lookout Point, with a view of the creek and marsh. Return to the junction at 2.1 miles and continue along the Maquam Creek Trail. The trail soon becomes more open and sunny as you enter the mowed roadway. Just past a wet spot in the roadway look for the junction (at 2.4 miles) of the road on which you entered. Turn left and hike back to Refuge Headquarters at 2.7 miles.

34

Belvidere Mountain

Total distance: 5.6 miles
Hiking time: 4.5 hours
Vertical rise: 2,140 feet
Rating: Moderately strenuous
Map: USGS 15' Jay Peak

Belvidere Mountain, famous for its asbestos mine, has a firetower which provides excellent views of northern Vermont.

The acquisition of 1,946 acres of land, including the summits of Belvidere Mountain, Haystack Mountain, and Tillotson Peak, is an important part of the Green Mountain Club's campaign to protect the Long Trail in northern Vermont. This valuable property embraces three miles of the Long Trail, four miles of side trails, Tillotson Camp, and Lockwood Pond. This significant purchase has protected valuable natural and trail resources, as well as helped the Club to move toward its overall goal of creating a protected corridor for the Long Trail.

To reach this trail, drive west on VT 118 from the junction of VT 100 and VT 118 in Eden (0.0) to a small four-car parking area at the Long Trail crossing, near the height of land at 4.9 miles. If you choose to park on the shoulder, be careful to park well off the road.

Begin your hike directly behind the parking area along the white-blazed Long Trail heading north. As you enter the woods, carefully follow the white blazes and avoid the numerous spur trails to the brook. You soon notice a trailer on the left, before you cross a

small clearing which was the former site of VT 118.

Enter the woods and begin a gradual climb parallel to the brook along an old road, occasionally leaving the road to avoid wet areas. At 1.0 mile the trail leaves the main road at a sharp right turn. Picking up other old roads, the trail climbs steeply, then continues over more rolling terrain through several wet areas.

By 1.3 miles you are into a series of rock shelves as the trail (sometimes on, sometimes parallel to old logging roads) continues to climb the west ridgeline. Descend slightly into a gully, climb up again, and cross a wet area on puncheon. Puncheon are small wooden bridges of one or more log or board planks held off the ground on sills. Begin another fairly steep ascent, and ignore any red blazes which mark a property line.

You soon reach a series of rock steps and switchbacks as you ascend a rocky portion of the trail. Cross another wet area on puncheon and come to a rock outcrop, at 2.1 miles, with views down the ridge. When the trail is wet, you can lose your footing on this rock outcrop, so keep to the uphill side for the easiest and safest route. Return to the woods

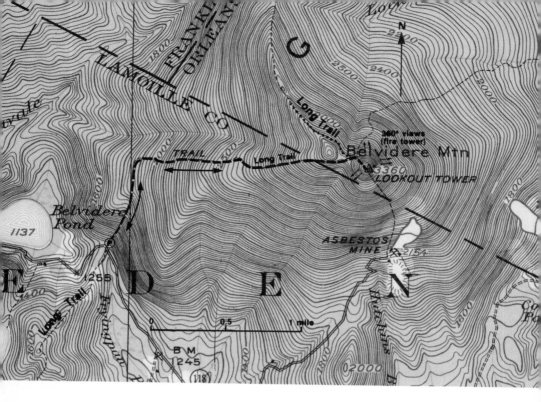

beyond the outcrop, continue your ascent across several wet areas and, as the trail levels somewhat, pass through a series of ridge plateaus.

At 2.6 miles you reach a trail junction. Straight ahead, the Forester's Trail descends to Tillotson Mill. To the left, the Long Trail continues along the ridge. You take the right hand trail to the summit of Belvidere Mountain. In 1919, a summit lookout station was established with the construction of a cabin, telephone lines, tower, and trail. In 1938, a hurricane blew down the old tower and a new steel tower was built. In 1968, a new trailer-type cabin was airlifted by helicopter to the summit. The tower was operated until about 1970, when airplane patrols replaced many firetowers. The current tower was renovated into a public lookout tower by the Green Mountain Club in 1982.

From the tower there are excellent views: to the north, Tillotson Peak and Haystack Mountain are in the foreground, with the summit station on Jay Peak directly behind Haystack, and Little Jay to the left; to the east, you can see the entire White Mountain Range from Mount Moosilauke, in the south, to the Presidentials in the north; to the southeast are Lake Eden, Green River Reservoir, and the Worcester Range from Mount Hunger to Elmore Mountain; to the southwest is the Green Mountain Range, including Mount Abraham, Camel's Hump, Mount Mansfield, Madonna Mountain, Whiteface Mountain, Butternut Mountain, and finally, Laraway Mountain; to the west are the Cold Hollow Range and the Adirondack Mountains.

After enjoying the views, use the same trails to return to your car.

35

Jay Peak

Total distance: 3.5 miles
Hiking time: 4 hours
Vertical rise: 1,680 feet
Rating: Moderate
Map: USGS 15' Jay Peak

Jay Peak

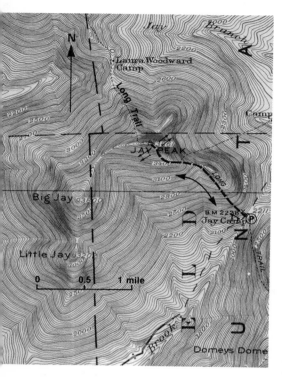

Jay Peak, the northernmost peak in the Green Mountain chain, was named in honor of John Jay, the first Chief Justice of the United States, who was instrumental in settling a controversy between the State of Vermont and the State of New York. Jay Peak, three miles of the Long Trail, and the Jay Peak Ski Area are all included in the 1,390-acre Jay State Forest. The forest is managed primarily for recreation, wildlife, and watershed protection. An enclosed aerial tramway at the Jay Peak Ski Area allows year-round visits to the summit, so expect a few other visitors.

The trailhead parking area for fifteen cars is at the height of land on the south side of VT 242, approximately 1.4 miles west of the Jay Peak Ski Area and 6.6 miles east of Montgomery Center.

Follow the white-blazed Long Trail north up the bank opposite the parking lot. At the beginning of the trail, you reach the Atlas Valley Shelter, a small lean-to made from plywood and plywood cores donated by the Atlas Valley Company. The shelter, not designed for overnight use, was prefabricated at the company's Morrisville plant and assembled on the site by members of the Green Mountain Club in 1967.

Continue your hike past the south end of a loop trail to Jay Camp, a frame cabin constructed in 1958 and maintained by the Green Mountain Club. Go straight at the junction, climb gradually, then more steeply through a hardwood forest, and pass the north end of the Jay Camp spur trail. Continue your ascent on the main trail through a birch grove, along the hillside, and across a field of birches and ferns. Turn left at 1.0 mile to avoid the ski area and hike over some steep ledges that parallel the ski trails. Turn left again at 1.2 miles and continue a steep climb until you emerge on a ski trail. Hike directly across the ski trail, enter the rocks, and climb steeply, at times rock scrambling, to the summit at 1.7 miles.

On the summit is the upper station of the Jay Peak Tramway. Please respect the buildings and property. On a clear day there are views of Canada to the north, the Adirondack Mountains to the west, the White Mountains to the east, and most of northern Vermont. The large lake to the northeast is Lake Memphremagog.

Hike back down the same way.

Tram ascending Jay Peak

36

Ritterbush Camp and Devil's Gulch

Total distance: 5 miles
Hiking time: 3 hours
Vertical rise: 1,040 feet
Rating: Moderate
Maps: USGS 15' Hyde Park, Jay Peak

This pleasant half-day hike takes you to Devil's Gulch, Ritterbush Camp, and Ritterbush Pond. Portions of the Long Trail in this area were recently acquired by the State of Vermont. More than ten miles of the Long Trail south from Ritterbush Pond, including Devil's Gulch, are now protected under state ownership through the efforts of The Nature Conservancy and the Green Mountain Club.

To reach the trail, look for a metal Long Trail sign on VT 118 between Eden and Belvidere at the height of land. The trailhead is approximately 4.9 miles from the VT 100/118 junction in Eden. Park on the wide shoulder or in the four-car parking area on the north side of the road.

From VT 118 follow the Long Trail south, up a bank, until you reach a registration box. Be sure to register, then continue your hike through overgrown farm pasture. After a short ascent, you reach a powerline cut with a view toward the east and VT 118. In the summer the fields and cleared powerline cut are filled with a variety of beautiful wild flowers.

Continue through a gully of young hardwoods, and begin a steep but short climb until you crest the ridge at 0.5

mile. The forest opens up from past logging activities as you hike uphill on a logging road through ferns and hardwoods. At 0.9 mile you begin a slight descent through more mixed hardwoods until you reach an overlook to Ritterbush Pond, a deep glacial cirque, at 1.5 miles.

The pond is part of the Babcock Nature Preserve, a natural area created in 1974. This tract of undeveloped wilderness was given to the Vermont State Colleges through The Nature Conservancy by Robert S. Babcock. The preserve includes 1,030 acres of mature, minimally disturbed, deciduous and mixed woodland with numerous streams, meadows, and three permanent ponds. Wildlife in the preserve includes the pygmy shrew (the world's smallest mammal), bobcats, bear, and moose. The preserve is also a prime birding location and the northernmost breeding locale of the Louisiana waterthrush. Big Muddy and Ritterbush ponds, as well as adjacent lands, are part of a watershed and three-year, nationally funded research study of forest nutrient dynamics and acid rain impact. Administration of the preserve is handled by Johnson State College.

Ritterbush Pond

The trail bears right at the overlook, begins a long steep descent utilizing log and stone steps, and parallels the edge of the hillside. At 1.9 miles you cross two small brooks and pass a spur trail on the right to Big Muddy Pond. Continue on the Long Trail over rolling terrain until you reach the edge of a long outcrop. Follow this outcrop, cross another brook, then swing right and climb up the face of a large rock outcrop to the camp. Ritterbush Camp, a frame building with bunks for about eight people, was constructed in 1933 and is maintained by the Laraway Section of the Green Mountain Club.

To reach Devil's Gulch, follow the Long Trail south behind the camp. The trail swings left, then right, and enters the gulch through a narrow passage in the rocks. Devil's Gulch, an interesting geological feature, is full of boulders and overgrown with ferns. Many different fern species can be found in the cool rock crevices and overhangs.

After enjoying this enchanting site, take the Long Trail north back to VT 118.

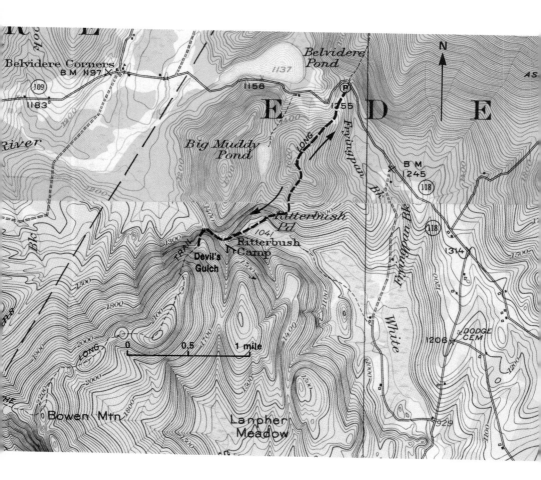

37

Elmore Mountain and Balanced Rock

Total distance: 4.5 miles
Hiking time: 3 hours
Vertical rise: 1,470 feet
Rating: Moderate
Map: USGS 7.5' Morrisville

Good views, a refurbished firetower, old stone foundations, a glacial boulder, and a beautiful lake at the foot of the mountain make this hike a wonderful choice for a day of outdoor activities in Elmore State Park.

The park, which charges a day use fee, began in 1933 when the town of Elmore deeded approximately thirty acres of land, including the beach on Lake Elmore, to the state. During the early 1940s, the Civilian Conservation Corps (CCC) constructed the bathhouse, picnic area, and a summit firetower and caretaker's cabin. The CCC was a government work program during the Great Depression of the 1930s.

The only public recreational facility in Lamoille County, the 706-acre park offers access to camping, a picnic area, hiking trails, swimming, boating, fishing, hunting, snowmobiling, cross-country skiing, and a winter weekend of dogsled racing. Lake Elmore is 204 acres in size and averages 8 feet deep, with a maximum depth of 15 feet. The lake is classified as a fair to good warm water fishing area. The fish species most sought after in Lake Elmore is northern pike. An abundant perch population has limited the numbers of other species.

Little Elmore Pond upstream has better quality fishing and is annually stocked with brown trout. While most of the park is forested, the steep terrain limits the availability of commercial timber.

Elmore State Park is located on VT 100 in Elmore. From the park entrance, drive left past the booth and into the woods. Follow the winding gravel road uphill 0.6 mile through the picnic area to a turn-around and parking area at the end of the road by the gate. The trail starts at the gate and continues on the gravel road.

Follow the gravel road to the top of the first grade, where a short spur on the right leads to a beaver pond. Continue on the road past a rock cut and then uphill to the end of the gravel road at 0.5 mile. At this point, the trail makes a sharp right turn, climbs the road bank on steps, and enters the woods. You follow a gully uphill with a small brook to your right as the trail ascends with occasional views of the lake on your left. Be sure to avoid the many spur trails in this section.

At 0.9 mile you switch back to the right and immediately make two steep ascents. At the top of the second ascent, pass through a rock cut and con-

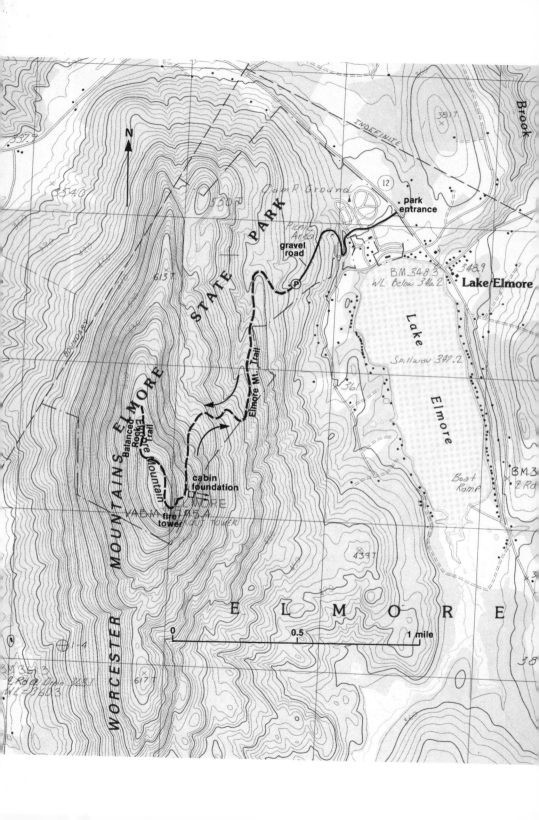

tinue over more level terrain. Next, cross a small brook on two logs, swing left, and ascend again. As you follow this gully upward, the trail looks very steep ahead. Don't worry, the trail bears left and begins a series of sweeping uphill switchbacks.

As you ascend the last long climb, white birches appear ahead, and at 1.4 miles you enter a clearing, the former site of the fire warden's cabin. The cabin was destroyed by an arsonist in 1982. All that remains is the foundation and chimney, yet the flowers planted by the warden near the foundation continue to bloom each spring and summer. From the clearing you have a good view down to the lake and the White Mountains to the east.

Continue your hike behind the cabin's former site and begin your final climb to the summit. Be careful not to slip into the spring, the original supply of water for the ranger's cabin. The summit climb is best described as a very steep scramble over rocks and roots!

At 1.7 mile you reach the junction of the Balanced Rock Trail noted by a blue arrow and "B.R." painted on a rock. Stay on the main trail and continue your hike a short distance to the tower, which is in excellent condition. It was abandoned as a firetower in the fall of 1974, but was repainted and repaired in 1987 by the State of Vermont.

Spectacular views from the tower in-clude the Worcester Range to the south, as well as the entire Green Mountain Range north from Camel's Hump, in-cluding Mount Mansfield, Laraway Mountain, Mount Belvidere (with the mine "scar"), and Jay Peak. To the west is the White Mountain chain from Mount Moosilauke to Mount Washington. The tower is also used by bird watchers every spring and fall, during hawk migrations.

After resting and enjoying the views, return to the Balanced Rock junction and follow this side trail along Elmore's ridge to a rock outcrop with beautiful views. The trail swings up and away from the east outcrop, climbs a shelf, and continues northwest over the ridge to a western outcrop. Follow along the ridge to the north behind the outcrop, descend slightly, and reach another outcrop with deep cracks created as weathered rock plates slid off the mountain. Be sure to enjoy the impressive views through these cracks. At 2.25 miles you reach Balanced Rock, a boulder left perched on the ridge by a glacier that receded during the last ice age.

Hike back to the junction and down the trail to your car. After completing your hike, cool off and refresh yourself with a swim in beautiful Lake Elmore. The lake is also a favorite site for local windsurfers; you may be able to rent a windsurfing board and give it a try!

38

Mount Pisgah

Total distance: 2.5 miles
Hiking time: 2–2.5 hours
Vertical rise: 1,590 feet
Rating: Moderate
Map: USGS 7.5′ Sutton Provisional

Mount Pisgah and Mount Hor (see hike 39) are located on Lake Willoughby and form the shear cliffs which descend to the lake. The cliffs have been designated a National Natural Landmark, as well as a Natural Area by the state of Vermont. Approximately 993 acres of the area are permanently protected. The geologic formation of Lake Willoughby and the adjacent cliffs area is unique and there are different interpretations of the formation process. The lake lies in a

Mount Pisgah (left) and Mount Hor across Lake Willoughby

Mount Pisgah as seen from Mount Hor

trough cut in granite by an exceptionally fine example of glacial scouring. Development, timber cutting, and road building are prohibited within the natural area.

The mountains are located in the 7,300-acre Willoughby State Forest, which was established in 1928. Much of the original purchase was once open farmland. In the 1930s the Civilian Conservation Corps, a government work program during the Depression, established plantations of Norway and white spruce, as well as red and white pine.

The forest includes hiking, cross-country skiing and snowmobile trails, and six small cold-water ponds that are annually stocked with brook and rainbow trout. Deer and grouse hunting are also popular within the forest.

Most of the trails in the area are still maintained by the Westmore Association and its associated Trails Committee. Although the association formed in 1967, some of the Westmore trails were laid out long before that time. Maintained by the association until 1989, the Mount Pisgah trails and the Mount Hor Trail

(Hawkes Trail—see hike 39) are now maintained by the state of Vermont.

Mount Pisgah is located on the east side of Lake Willoughby. The trail parallels a steep rock face with great views down to the lake, Burke Mountain, and the surrounding area. The original "south" trail up Pisgah dates back to the late 1800s.

To reach the Mount Pisgah trailhead from the south, drive 5.7 miles north on VT 5A from the intersection of VT 5 and VT 5A in West Burke (0.0) to the parking area on the left (west) side of the road before Lake Willoughby.

To reach the trailhead from the north or east, drive east on VT 16 from the center of Barton (0.0) to the intersection of VT 16 and VT 5 at 0.3 mile. Turn left on VT 16 and continue to the VT 5A intersection at 7.3 miles. Turn right (south) on VT 5A to the parking area on the right (west) side of the road at 13.0 miles. As you drive along the east side of Lake Willoughby, you can see Mount Hor on the right and Mount Pisgah on the left.

The parking area for twenty cars has picnic tables for a lunch or snack, plus a signboard about the area trails. The trailhead sign on the opposite side of the road indicates a distance of 1.7 miles to the summit of Mount Pisgah.

Cross the road from the parking area and descend the road embankment on the blue-blazed trail until you come to a swamp. Avoid the faint blue blazes to the right. Instead, turn left and cross an unusual wooden bridge over the swamp. You can see occasional views of the Mount Hor cliffs. Climb the bank behind the pond and follow an old road which bears right away from the pond.

As you start to see a clearing ahead, the trail makes a sharp left and begins a long switchback climb. Look for a water pipe along the trail, and take time to notice the extensive maintenance work required in this area. You soon follow the ridge uphill on a wide, more gradual trail. To the left is the steep side of the mountain descending to Lake Willoughby. At 0.9 mile a small sign indicates the spur trail to Pulpit Rock. Here, you find an excellent view down to the lake and Mount Hor beyond. Be careful—you are standing on a rock overhang, approximately 550 feet above the lake.

Back on the main trail, continue a steady climb along the ridge and then bear right. Moving away from the lake, you enter a maple forest, ascend the hillside, and hike through a birch forest. As the trail gets narrower, climb through boulders and skirt a ledge at 1.3 mile. You have now lost all views of the lake as you enter a softwood forest along the backside of the mountain.

The trail switches back until you find yourself at the bottom of a long rock slab. Climb the slab for a good view of the Burke Mountain area. Above the slab, you enter the woods and reach a side trail leading to East Overlook. Continue down along the ridge until, at 1.9 miles, you reach a spur trail on the left to the Upper Overlook. Take this steep, muddy trail down to a spectacular view of Lake Memphremagog, Lake Willoughby, Wheeler Mountain, Mount Hor, Jay Peak, the Green Mountain Range, and the surrounding area.

Return to the trail junction and hike back down the main trail to your car.

39

Mount Hor

Total distance: 3.5 miles
Hiking time: 3 hours
Vertical rise: 1,050 feet
Rating: Easy to moderate
Map: USGS 7.5' Sutton

Lake Willoughby from Mount Hor

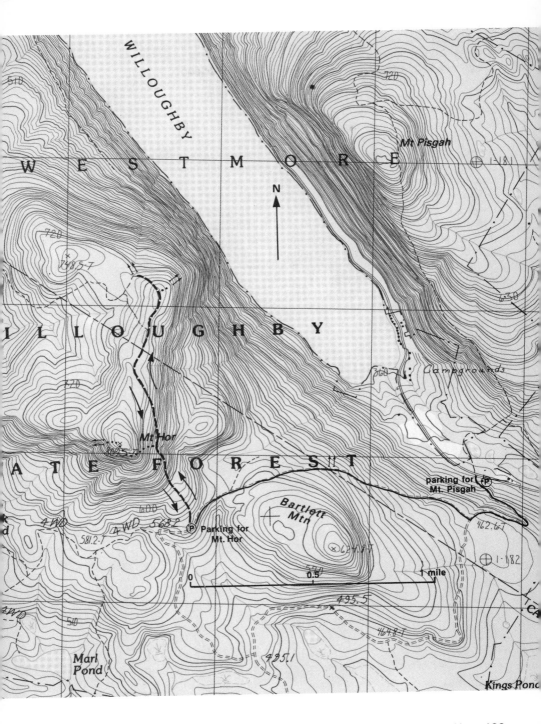

Mount Hor is located to the west of Lake Willoughby (see hike 38 for information on Willoughby State Forest). The summit is wooded, but the trail goes to two vantage points on the cliffs, with beautiful views of the lake below. The Mount Hor Trail is now called the Herbert and Evelyn Hawkes Trail in honor of two members of the Westmore Association who laid out the trail to the mountain summit and overlook.

To reach the Mount Hor trailhead, follow the directions to the Mount Pisgah parking area (hike 38) and then proceed up the narrow gravel road at the right side of the parking area (0.0). Bear right at the fork. Continue up the road to a small parking area for five cars on the right at 1.8 miles. A sign just past the parking area on the right side of the road marks the blue-blazed trail up Mount Hor.

Climb the bank and follow an old road to the right. There are very few blazes on the small maple trees, so please be careful to stay on the trail.

At 0.4 mile you begin a hillside walk through maples and nettles. As you approach the top of the maple grove, the trail swings left and across a series of switchbacks until you reach a trail junction at 0.7 mile.

From this junction, hike uphill on the serpentine, overgrown, and only faintly blazed West Branch Trail to the wooded summit of Mount Hor. Just beyond the summit is an overlook of Bean, Wheeler, Blake, Duck and Vail Ponds, as well as Burke Mountain.

Return to the trail junction and follow the East Branch/Wheeler Pond Trail along the ridge line to the overlooks above Lake Willoughby. You soon reach a trail junction. Do not take the Wheeler Pond Trail, which turns left and descends five miles to the pond. Continue on the East Branch Trail along the ridge to the junction of the East Lookout Trail on the right. Descend on the East Lookout Trail to an overlook of the lake. An even better lookout is found by going a little farther down the ridge to the north lookout, which overlooks Lake Willoughby and Mount Pisgah beyond. This lookout, with its breathtaking views, is a breezy place to stop for lunch.

Return to the summit to hike back down to the trailhead.

Mount Hunger

Total distance: 4 miles
Hiking time: 3.5–4 hours
Vertical rise: 2,330 feet
Rating: Moderately strenuous
Map: USGS 7.5' Stowe

This hike goes to the open south summit of Mount Hunger. The 3,539-foot summit provides excellent views of the Green Mountain chain and the White Mountains of New Hampshire. Mount Hunger is part of the Worcester chain, which begins near the Winooski River and ends at Elmore Mountain to the north.

To reach Mount Hunger take VT 100 to Waterbury Center and turn east (0.0) on the road to "Waterbury Center P.O./Loomis Hill/Barnes Hill." (This turn is 0.3 mile south of the Cold Hollow Cider Mill.) Drive straight 0.3 mile and turn left (north) onto Maple Street. Just past the fire station, at 0.4 mile, turn right onto Loomis Hill Road, which turns to dirt at 2.3 miles. Bear left at the top of Loomis Hill Road and continue on Loomis Hill Road until you reach a parking area for ten to fifteen cars on the right at 3.8 miles. A post and sign identify the trailhead, which is also the site where stones were crushed during construction of the interstate.

The trail begins behind the parking area and passes through the remains of the crusher site. There are no blazes at this point, but the trail is obvious. Blue blazes appear as the trail enters the woods and begins a series of switchbacks through huge, moss-covered boulders. Numerous old logging roads intersect the trail. Cross a gully and resume your climb along a ridge with numerous rock outcrops. At 0.5 mile the trail levels, you cross a small brook, and begin a long climb along a moderate slope.

Look for a large white birch, which indicates the end of the long hill. Turn right and descend along the hillside into a moss-covered, rock strewn valley that provides cool, welcome relief on a hot summer day.

Cross the valley floor and a small brook. Look for a large boulder field upstream. Continue uphill through birches until you meet an old trail at 1.0 mile. Turn left and follow switchbacks up the hillside with several views back into the valley. You soon cross another brook and enter a stand of stately white birches. Climb through the loose rocks and roots until you find a nice large rock on the left at 1.4 miles. This site is a good place to rest. Continue your hike along a more level trail and by a brook. The trail enters a hemlock stand and becomes steeper as you pass over large rocks with limited views to the west. At 1.8 miles you reach the junction of the

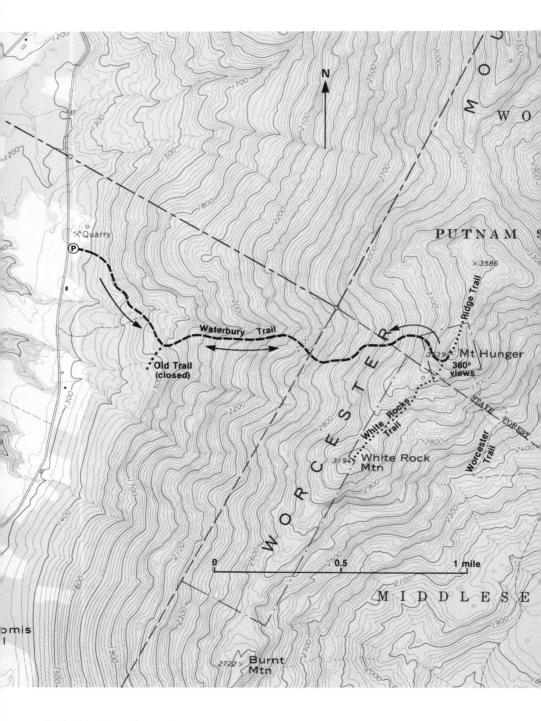

Quarry

P

Waterbury Trail

Old Trail
(closed)

PUTNAM S

×3586

Ridge Trail

Mt Hunger
360°
views

WORCESTER

White Rocks Trail

White Rock
Mtn

STATE FOREST

Worcester Trail

0   0.5   1 mile

MIDDLESE

Burnt
Mtn

omis

Summit of Mount Hunger

White Rock Trail, which branches to the right.

From the junction, continue on the main trail, which steeply ascends a short distance to a view of White Rock Mountain. As you near the summit, you scramble over rocks to the south summit of Mount Hunger. Be sure to avoid the blue-blazed Worcester Trail, which descends the other side of the ridge. Another trail also heads north to the wooded north summit and continues on to Stowe Pinnacle.

The south summit offers spectacular views of Waterbury Reservoir, Camel's Hump, White Rock Mountain, Mount Mansfield, the White Mountains, the Worcester range, and area valleys. Enjoy the patterns created by the roads, fields, forests, ponds, and rivers below you.

After you rest and enjoy the view, take the same trail back to your car.

Stowe Pinnacle

Total distance: 2.8 miles
Hiking time: 2 hours
Vertical rise: 1,520 feet
Rating: Moderate
Map: USGS 7.5' Stowe

Stowe Pinnacle

This short, occasionally steep hike up a rocky knob offers you great views of the entire Worcester Range, as well as the Green Mountain Range, the Waterbury Reservoir, and the surrounding area.

To reach the trail, take VT 100 to the Village of Stowe and turn east (0.0) on School Street. At 0.3 mile bear right at the fork on the Stowe Hollow Road. At 1.8 miles the road reaches an intersection, where you go straight on the Upper Hollow Road. The road crosses a brook and turns to gravel. Continue uphill, bear right, pass Pinnacle Road, and at 2.5 miles reach a state parking lot for eight cars on the left (east) side of the road.

The blue-blazed trail, which starts at

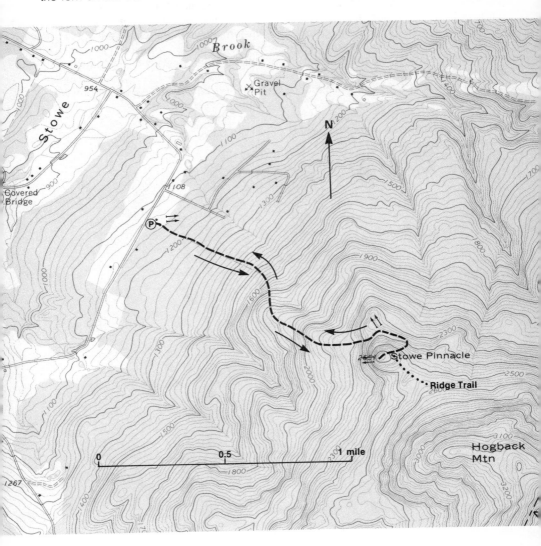

the back of the narrow parking lot, begins by crossing a field and overgrown pasture. Both the Worcester Range and Stowe Pinnacle are directly in front of you. You soon pass by a large boulder and young mixed hardwoods. The trail becomes quite rocky and begins to ascend. At 0.4 mile cross through a gully, turn right, cross another gully, and begin a steeper climb through mature hardwoods. A sharp right turn leads you up onto a plateau. The trail swings left at 0.8 mile and you scramble over rocks into a notch. As you reach the top of the notch, a short spur trail on the left leads to a view of Mount Mansfield and the Stowe area.

After enjoying the view, return to the junction and follow the main trail behind the ridge you just climbed. The trail descends slightly and then resumes its climb up the pinnacle. As you gain elevation, the trail is rockier and short fir trees indicate you are getting closer to the summit. A trail enters from the left that leads to the Worcester Ridge and Hunger Mountain. The Pinnacle Trail bears right and at 1.4 miles you climb out onto the pinnacle with eastern views of the Worcester Range from Hunger Mountain to Mount Elmore. There are western views of the Green Mountain Range including, from south to north, Mounts Ethan and Ira Allen, Camel's Hump, Bolton Mountain, Mount Mansfield, and Whiteface Mountain. The Waterbury Reservoir can also be seen in the foreground.

Hike back down the same trail to your car.

Sawmill Loop—Little River State Park

Total distance: 2.5 miles
Hiking time: 2 hours
Vertical rise: 650 feet
Rating: Easy
Map: USGS 7.5' Bolton Mountain

Little River Sawmill Trail

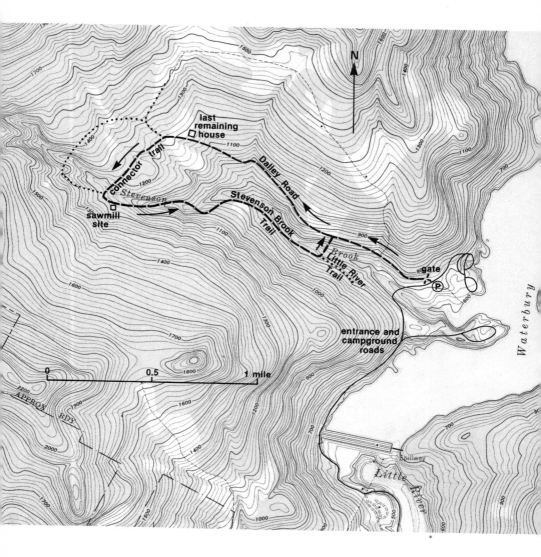

Little River State Park, established in 1962, is a 1,100-acre park located in the 37,000 acre Mount Mansfield State Forest. The park's Waterbury Dam was completed in 1938 by the U.S. Army Corps of Engineers and the Civilian Conservation Corps (CCC), after two serious floods of the Little River in 1927 and 1934. The CCC was a government work program during the Great Depression of the 1930s.

This hike leads you to abandoned settlements with stone walls, cemeteries, old roads, foundations, orchards, and more. You are welcome to photograph the area and any artifacts you find, but please do not remove any items from the park.

To reach the park, drive west on US 2 from the junction of US 2 and VT 100 in Waterbury (0.0). At 1.4 miles turn right (north) on the road to the Little River State Park. Go under the interstate and continue to the Waterbury Dam at 4.2 miles. The road bears left, ascends the bank of the dam, and at 4.5 miles reaches the Park entrance. A day use fee is charged. Pass the entry station, and drive down and across a bridge at 5.0 miles. Go past the "Nature Trail" parking area at the bridge, and park in a small parking area on the right, across from a gated road.

To begin your hike, cross the main road and climb up the gated Dalley Road. Listen for the Stevenson Brook as you hike gradually uphill along the gravel roadway. Almost immediately, you reach the Hedgehog Hill Trail junction on the right. Continue on the road and notice several old stone walls, which indicate the area was once used for pasture land. The Little River Trail, on which you return, enters on the left.

At 0.6 mile you enter a hemlock grove, descend slightly, and cross a brook. After you pass a gravel pit and climb uphill, you reach the Almeron Goodell Farmhouse. This house is the only remaining farmhouse in the Little River area. Disabled Civil War veteran Almeron Goodell was, according to one story, an escaped slave adopted by an area Goodell family. He bought the land around 1864 and built the house of hewn timbers and hand-split shingles.

The trail continues past the house, across the brook, and up the road. Look for old apple orchards and maybe even some old farm machinery. As you enter a stand of birches, you reach the Stevenson Brook Trail junction on the left.

The blue-blazed trail, which is not well maintained, leaves the road and descends through the birches and ferns to Stevenson Brook. As you cross a small brook, you find old stone walls and the remains of an old road crossing. Climb the brook bank and hike along the old roadway, which is easy to follow despite a lack of blazes. As you enter some hemlocks, descend to the steep bank of Stevenson Brook. Just before you reach the bank, the trail turns left to a brook crossing. Be extremely careful on the slippery rocks, especially when the water level is high. Ascend an old roadway up the opposite bank.

At 1.4 miles you reach a trail junction. Take the trail to the right, which leads to the remains of the Waterbury Last Block Co. Sawmill. This steam-powered band sawmill was constructed in 1917 and operated until 1922. The mill, run by two 150-horsepower boilers, employed thirty-five men, forty-four horse teams, and one truck. The timber was used for ammunition cases and gun stocks, while the finer wood was hauled to Waterbury for cobblers' "lasts" (shoe molds). Now, only the large boiler, truck chassis, and band saws remain.

Pass the mill and bear left on an overgrown roadway. During the summer, the first part of the trail is a continuous nettle patch. The old road widens as you descend along Stevenson Brook and reach the abutments of old road bridges. At 1.75 miles you cross one brook and then another. As you walk along the old road, look for evidence of former settlements. You soon enter some hemlocks and go slightly downstream to a brook crossing. Look for an old roadway ascending the opposite bank. Take this old road, called the Little River Trail, until it intersects the Dalley Road. Take a right and follow the Dalley Road back to your car at 2.5 miles.

History Loop—Groton State Forest

Total distance: 4 miles
Hiking time: 4 hours
Vertical rise: 560 feet
Rating: Easy to moderate
Map: USGS 15' Plainfield

Groton State Forest is one of the most popular recreational areas in northern Vermont. The forest has been used since the early 1890s for hunting, swim- ming, boating, hiking, fishing, berry picking, skiing, and more recently for snowmobiling. Because the land was too rocky to farm, area residents used

Old mill site on Groton history hike

the region's forests of spruce, hemlock, beech, birch, maple, and white pine for fuel, lumber, and making potash for fertilizer and soap.

Since acquiring the first tract of land in 1919, the State of Vermont now owns approximately 25,000 acres in Groton State Forest. The Civilian Conservation Corps (CCC) planted trees and was instrumental in the construction of roads, hiking trails, picnic shelters, and stone fireplaces. The CCC was a government work program during the Great Depression. Groton State Forest is now managed by the Vermont Department of Forests, Parks and Recreation for summer and winter recreation, forestry, and as a wildlife habitat.

To reach the forest, drive north on US 2 from Marshfield Village (0.0) to the junction of VT 232 at 1.0 mile. Turn east on VT 232 and drive past the New Discovery Campground entrance at 5.3 miles. At 9.4 miles turn left to Lake Groton and continue past the Stillwater Camping Area and the end of Lake Groton. The road turns to dirt and you pass the Big Deer Campground. At 11.1 miles turn left and park at the Nature Center.

Be sure to stop at the Center and pick up a copy of the "Groton State Forest History Guide" and the "Groton State Forest Guide to Trails," to supplement this description. This four mile hike allows for several other short hikes to points of interest described in these free pamphlets.

Begin your hike at the back of the Nature Center parking lot on the blue-blazed Coldwater Brook Trail. After climbing the bank behind the lot, follow the relatively flat, wide trail through a softwood forest over a very soft treadway. At 0.4 mile you reach a trail junction. Descend the Coldwater Brook Trail

to a small ridge which drops off to the brook below.

At 0.9 mile be careful not to lose the trail, as you intersect a logging road. Turn right on the road, continue for about twenty-five yards, then turn left, back onto the trail. You soon cross another logging road, which the trail follows for a short distance, before returning to the woods. Continue your hike through a wet area and across a brook on rocks. At 1.1 miles stop at the foundations of an old mill along Coldwater Brook. This waterwheel-powered mill is believed to have been a small up-and-down sawmill that operated before the Civil War.

The trail follows the brook upstream, then moves away from the brook and makes a sharp left turn. After the turn, enter a more open area, which indicates previous logging activity. The trail continues along a gully, crosses a brook, and passes through an unusual, small meadow of rocks surrounded by ferns. Watch your step around the rocks.

At 1.9 miles you reach a trail junction and side trail to Big Deer Mountain. This one mile loop is described in the forest trail guide. From the junction take the Osmore Pond Trail across a wet area and through some ferns. Crest a small knoll, cross an old logging road, and descend along another old roadway. At 2.3 miles you are at the south end of Osmore Pond and another trail junction. A right turn takes you two miles around the pond and back to the trail junction.

Continue left and follow the Hosmer Brook Trail, which descends parallel to the brook. Although scenic in this section, the trail is quite rocky, so be sure to watch your step. At 2.8 miles leave the brook and enter the woods. You pass a very large boulder and walk through a boulder field back to the

brook. You soon enter a hemlock stand to avoid a wet area and return to a boulder field among birches. As you begin to hear sounds of civilization, a steep bank appears on the left. At 3.7 miles the trail reaches the main park road at a power transformer. Turn left on the road, pass the entrance to Big Deer Campground on the left, and continue to the Nature Center entrance and your car at 4.0 miles.

Spruce Mountain

Total distance: 4.5 miles
Hiking time: 3 hours
Vertical rise: 1,340 feet
Rating: Moderate
Map: USGS 7.5' East Barre

This trail leads to an abandoned firetower, as well as several lookouts with
excellent views of north and central Vermont and western New Hampshire. Children especially enjoy exploring a very
large split rock 1.6 miles along the trail.

Most of the trail up Spruce Mountain
is located in the L. R. Jones State Forest, a 642-acre parcel of land located in
Plainfield. This forest, the first parcel
purchased by the State of Vermont, on
November 24, 1909, was formerly called
the Plainfield State Forest. The name
was changed to L. R. Jones State Forest in honor of Professor L. R. Jones, a
University of Vermont Professor of Bot-
any, in recognition of his efforts to establish the State Tree Nursery and
create the position of State Forester. The
summit of Spruce Mountain is located in
Groton State Forest.

To reach the trail, take US 2 to Plainfield. Turn south at the flashing yellow
light (0.0), cross a bridge, and bear left.
At 0.4 mile turn right on East Hill Road,
which quickly turns to gravel. At 2.0
miles Spruce Mountain is visible ahead.
At 3.6 miles cross a small bridge and
go straight. As you go downhill at 4.3
miles, turn left. At 4.7 miles bear left at
a bend in the now twisty and bumpy

road. At 5.4 miles turn right and drive
past the site of the old gate and parking
area to a new parking area for ten to fifteen cars and a second gate. Please
park in this upper lot, which is located
on state rather than private land.

Begin your hike along the roadway
past the gate. During this one-mile road
walk, notice the frequent views of
Spruce Mountain; the fragrant spruce-
scented air; and in the fall, a few beautiful, full-color maple trees along the way.
Also, look for ruffed grouse in the
woods—you may startle one into sudden flight. Although numerous old logging roads intersect the roadway, be
sure to stay on the main road. Don't be
concerned that you appear to be walking away from Spruce Mountain.

At 1.0 mile, a wooden sign indicates
that the trail and road bear left. You
soon cross an unusual area of small,
round rocks, or as one hiker describes
it, "a baby boulder field," where the road
ends. The relatively level, rocky trail
continues past a large boulder engulfed
by the roots of a birch tree. You soon
cross a brook on puncheon, a small
wooden bridge of one or more logs or
board planks held off the ground on
sills. At 1.5 miles turn right and climb a

switchback to avoid an old eroded part of the trail. The ascent is quite steep. The trail finally levels somewhat and you reach a large rock outcrop split by the freezing and thawing of water. This is a good place to take a break and explore the rock.

The trail continues past the rock and ascends along a hillside by the bottom edge of a sloping, exposed rock slab. Follow the slab until 1.9 miles where you swing right for a steeper ascent.

The trail returns to a mix of hard and softwoods, and enters a small open area of ferns before returning to the woods. Bear right into a rocky area on your left and continue until you reach an overlook on the right.

Immediately to the left of the overlook is the summit, with an abandoned firetower and the remains of a ranger's cabin. The original tower was built in 1919 and used until 1931, when the tower was replaced and the cabin was

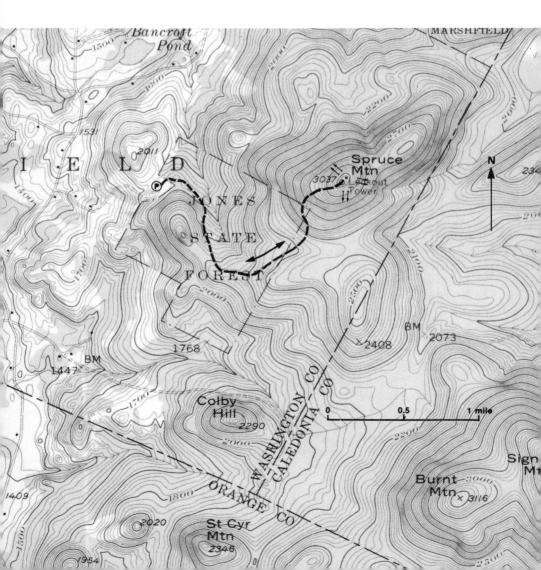

Spruce Mountain Trail

built. In 1943, the current steel lookout tower was transferred to Spruce Mountain from Bellevue Hill near St. Albans. The tower, which has not been used as a firetower since around 1974, was repainted and repaired in 1987.

A rock outcrop on the summit provides a nice view of Groton State Forest, including Pigeon and Noyes Ponds. From the tower, enjoy extensive views of central Vermont, the Green Mountain Range, and western New Hampshire.

After enjoying the views, hike back down the same trail to your car.

Sterling Pond and Elephant's Head

Total distance: 6.0 miles
Hiking time: 4 hours
Vertical rise: 1,780 feet
Rating: Strenuous
Map: USGS 7.5' Mount Mansfield

This trail begins in Smugglers Notch, a beautiful passageway between Mount Mansfield and Sterling Peak. Smugglers Notch was a favorite route for smuggling goods into and out of Canada. In 1807, northern Vermonters faced a serious hardship when President Jefferson passed an embargo act. The act forbade American trade with Great Britain and Canada. Because Montreal was such a close and lucrative market, many Vermonters continued illegal trade with Canada by herding cattle and transporting other goods through the notch. The notch was also used by fugitive slaves as an escape route to Canada, and by Vermonters in the 1920s to smuggle liquor from Canada during prohibition.

The rocks of the notch were formed about 400 million years ago, when the land was at the bottom of a shallow sea. Clay particles, sand, and animal shells drifted to the sea floor and eventually were pressed into shale-type rocks. About 100 million years later, the land was pushed up to form the Green Mountains. The sedimentary rocks were subjected to tremendous pressure and high temperatures, which rearranged the minerals into the banded patterns you see today. This "metamorphosed"

rock, called schist, is primarily composed of the minerals mica, albite, and quartz, and occasionally garnet, magnetite, and chlorite.

Although geologists are not certain how the notch was formed, most believe that it was carved by a southward flowing river. Twelve thousand years ago, as the first glacier was retreating, the ice on the eastern side of the Green Mountains probably melted first. The glacier remained on the western side and blocked the melt-water from flowing west. Thus, a river of melted ice rushed through the notch, down into the Stowe area.

The magnificent cliffs of the notch contain shapes which resemble other objects. With a little imagination you can find the Smuggler's Face, Singing Bird, Elephant's Head, and the Hunter and His Dog. The cliffs also contain some of the rarest and most endangered plants in Vermont. The constantly dripping water in the cliff's cracks breaks down the rock minerals and nourishes the few plants that manage to grow in the cracks. The combination of a steep face where few plants can survive, a cold microclimate, and a constant supply of mineral-rich water create a very unusual

Old Smugglers Face

Smugglers Cave ○

r Pond

Long Trail

Smugglers Notch

Elephants
Head

1803

Big Spring

road walk

MATE BOUNDARY

Elephants Head Trail

State
picnic
area

108

TRAIL

LONG

N

MSFIELD STATE

FOREST

Tower ○

SKI LIFT

Barnes Camp

State Ski Dormitory

The Pinnacle

Spruce Peak

Lodge

Long Trail

Sterling Pond

Sterling Pond
Loop

THE

APPROXIMATE

APPROX

LONG

M O R

N

0   0.5   1 mile

set of environmental factors. This plant community is called a Cold Calcareous Cliff Community. Please do not disturb or pick any plants in the notch.

To reach Smugglers Notch, take VT 108, the Stowe-Jeffersonville Highway, 10 miles north of Stowe or 8 miles south of Jeffersonville. Park in the lot at the top of the notch. Be sure to review the information on the parking area bulletin board. A short distance to the left of the parking area and information booth is Smuggler's Cave, an alleged hiding place for smuggled goods during the War of 1812.

From the parking area, cross the road and take the white-blazed Long Trail north. Read the information board at the beginning of the trail. Start your hike up a steep ascent on stone steps, across a drainage gully, and along a plateau. To the left are views down the steep bank into the notch, and ahead is a large rock outcrop. The trail ascends steeply to the right. A log bench at the top provides a welcome spot to rest.

Continue your climb on moderate to steep grades up the hillside, through softwoods and a series of plateaus with occasional views along the way. At 0.8 mile you reach a ski trail that connects the Sterling and Spruce Peak lifts. Turn left and follow the wide ski trail down to the outlet of Sterling Pond. You can see Madonna Mountain across the pond.

Surrounded by boreal forest, Sterling Pond is spring-fed, stocked with trout, and relatively shallow, although beaver dams have increased the depth of the pond. Originally a large talc deposit, the pond formed after the last glacier cut a depression in the talc. There are still talc deposits along the trail which, by the way, are very slippery. At one time, a talc mine was considered, but disregarded because the pond was too remote.

For a short side trip, take a left on the Long Trail across the pond outlet and around the pond to Sterling Pond Shelter. In front of the shelter, take a right on the Elephant's Head Trail, hike past Watson Camp, and continue back to the pond outlet. Due to the popularity of this area, a Green Mountain Club Caretaker is stationed at Watson Camp during the hiking season.

To continue your hike, turn right at the pond outlet and ascend the blue-blazed Elephant's Head Trail up a steep bank. The trail quickly ascends to an overlook of the pond. Cross a wet area and, as you ascend again, be sure to enjoy the views. At 1.2 miles you reach the junction of a blue-blazed trail that circles the pond. Turn right at the junction and continue on the Elephant's Head Trail. You first cross a knob with views of Mount Mansfield, and then you cross a ski trail. Go straight across the ski trail and reenter the woods. Swing west around Spruce Peak, and enjoy good views across the notch. Watch your step as you hike down a series of very steep pitches.

At 2.2 miles you reach the spur trail to the top of Elephant's Head. Turn right on the spur trail and begin a steep descent to the top of Elephant's Head at 2.3 miles. From the cliff summit, you can see 1,000 feet straight down to the roadway below you. Across the notch are the sheer walls of Mount Mansfield and the scar left by the 1983 landslide.

Because peregrine falcons have recently returned to the Elephant's Head cliff, the trail to the top of Elephant's Head may be closed during their nesting season. These beautiful, endangered birds are extremely sensitive to human disturbance, especially from above. Please obey all trail signs during nesting season, and see the introduction for more information about the falcons.

Sterling Pond

Follow the spur trail back to the main trail and turn right at the junction. The trail becomes quite steep as you hike and sometimes crawl up and down the hillside on exposed rocks and roots. Be very careful of your footing. Expect to lower yourself occasionally over rock outcrops. This trail is very rugged, but quite beautiful and worth the extra effort.

The trail begins a switchback to the right as birches appear and the grade is easier. As you cross the 1985 rock and mud slide at 3.3 miles, notice how thin the soils are along the slide at this elevation. Enter the woods, complete another long switchback, and cross the lower portion of the slide. Continue downhill on more moderate grades through a mixed forest of birch and maple. The trail narrows, passes over a rock ledge at 3.8 miles, and soon gets steep again. Descend a long grade, swing right, and cross two brooks. Pass by the picnic area outhouse and turn right to the picnic area at 4.5 miles.

Continue your hike along VT 108, through the notch, back to the parking area. Along the way, observe the lower portion of the slide you previously crossed. At 5.3 miles you reach Big Spring, a nice place to stop for a well-deserved drink. Hike through the hairpin turns and among the boulders, which have fallen into the notch, back to your car at 6.0 miles.

Weekend Backpacking Hikes

Glastenbury Mountain and West Ridge Loop

Total distance: 21.8 mile loop
Hiking time: 2 days, 1 night
Vertical rise: 3,640 feet
Rating: Strenuous
Maps: GMNF Woodford, Bennington

There are few opportunities on Vermont's Long Trail for loop backpacking trips. This hike, through remote forests and over several mountains, is an excellent exception.

Your first day follows the Long Trail and Appalachian Trails (LT/AT) north from VT 9 through a very isolated forest to Goddard Shelter and the summit of Glastenbury Mountain. A summit firetower provides spectacular views of southern Vermont.

The second day, you hike south on the West Ridge Trail to the summit of Bald Mountain and then back to VT 9.

The trailhead is on the north side of VT 9, 5.2 miles east of Bennington and approximately one mile west of Woodford.

Day One

Total distance: 10.1 miles
Hiking time: 6 hours
Vertical rise: 2,640 feet

From the parking area, take the white-blazed LT/AT north, parallel to and then across City Stream on the William A. McArthur Bridge. The bridge was built in 1977 by the United States Forest Ser-

vice (USFS) in memory of a Green Mountain Club member who helped to maintain the trails in this area. Follow the stream a short distance, bear right, and begin a very steep ascent up the ridgeline. You can still see evidence of the small tornado which devastated this hillside in 1988. Utilizing a series of rocky switchbacks, you climb rapidly out of the VT 9 valley.

At 0.6 mile you pass through a split rock before you begin a moderate ascent. Cross two old roads, first a small one, and then a larger one at 1.1 miles. You soon reach a spur trail on the right at 1.7 miles, which leads 200 feet to the Melville Nauheim Shelter. The shelter, constructed in 1977 by the Bennington Section of the Green Mountain Club, is a good place to rest.

Return to the trail junction and continue north over slightly easier grades to a powerline cut on Maple Hill at 2.0 miles. Take time to enjoy the views of Bennington and Mount Anthony to the west, Mount Snow and Haystack Mountain to the east. Continue uphill to the top of Maple Hill and then descend across a wet area on puncheon. Puncheon are small wooden bridges of one or more log or board planks held

off the ground on sills. Now on rolling terrain, the trail leads you across Hell Hollow Brook on a bridge at 3.1 miles. Camping is not permitted in this area because the brook is part of the Bennington public water supply.

Beyond the brook, continue your ascent across a swamp filled with balsam and spruce trees, and up the ridge to a lookout at 4.3 miles. The lookout is a nice place to stop for lunch while gazing across the valley to Haystack Mountain.

After lunch, continue on rolling terrain over two hills to the 3,100-foot summit of Little Pond Mountain at 5.5 miles and Little Pond Lookout. With Glastenbury Mountain still in the distance, you climb over two minor summits and along the ridgeline to Glastenbury Lookout at 7.4 miles. From this overlook you see the summit of Glastenbury ahead, your destination for the first day. Descend into and then out of an overgrown sag. The trail soon gets very steep as you climb the mountain on steps. Cross a spring and reach Goddard Shelter at 9.8 miles.

Goddard Shelter, the third shelter at the same site on Glastenbury, was built in 1985. The first shelter was built of tin in 1929, and the second of logs in 1965. In 1983, Ted Goddard, Jr., made a generous financial offer to help build a new shelter in 1983, in memory of his father. Almost all the materials were cut on site, but because the native balsam fir trees were not in the best health, dimension lumber for flooring and roofing materials had to be airlifted to the site by the Air National Guard.

After you settle in and eat dinner, take a short, 0.3-mile trip to the wooded summit of Glastenbury Mountain. The firetower, built in 1927 by the Vermont Timberland Owners' Association, was abandoned in the late 1940s and later renovated by the USFS as an observation deck for hikers. From the tower, you have a breathtaking 360-degree view of the surrounding wilderness. You can see Mount Equinox and Stratton Mountain to the north; Haystack Mountain, Mount Snow, and the Somerset Reservoir to the east. Return to the shelter for a much-needed and welcome good night's rest.

Day Two

Total distance: 11.7 miles
Hiking time: 7 hours
Vertical rise: 1,000 feet

If you are an early riser, climb the summit tower to enjoy a spectacular sunrise and a blanket of mist in the valley below. Eat breakfast, load your pack, and look for the blue-blazed West Ridge Trail just west of the shelter. Take this initially obscure trail down the western ridge of the mountain. Bear left and continue your descent with limited views back to Glastenbury Mountain and of the valley below. There are very few blazes along this hillside, so be sure to stay on the trail.

Ascend over a crest, then begin a long descent to an old logging road where you turn right, walk a few yards, and turn left back into the woods. Hike around a beaver pond, and up to a major logging road at 2.5 miles. Turn right on the road, walk a few yards, turn left up the steep bank, and begin a very long, steep climb to a 3,423-foot minor summit. As you hike along the ridge, the blazes are easier to follow. Pass through a stand of dense hemlocks, then return to mixed hardwoods and a more open forest. The trail is quite rocky as you hike along the hillside.

The summit of Bald Mountain is reached at 7.7 miles. Although wooded, the summit is long and flat, with numerous views and light-colored rocks.

Trail up Glastenbury Mountain

Try to spot the route you just hiked between Glastenbury Mountain (with the firetower) and Bald Mountain. Enjoy views to the south of Mount Greylock and to the west of the Taconic Mountain Range.

The West Ridge Trail ends at a junction with the Bald Mountain Trail. A right turn leads east to Bennington. You turn left on the Bald Mountain Trail and begin a steep, rocky descent to a USFS trail sign and spur trail to Bear Wallow (a spring). The trail now follows an old road which is intersected by numerous old logging roads. At the red-blazed USFS boundary, turn right and descend along the roadway. You pass a register box and start to see signs of civilization. At 9.7 miles you reach the Bald Mountain trailhead parking area and a public road. Turn right and follow the road to VT 9 in Woodford Hollow at 10.5 miles. Turn left on VT 9 and hike back to your car in the LT/AT parking area at 11.7 miles.

VT 118 to VT 242

Total distance: 17.5 miles
Hiking time: 2 days, 1 night
Vertical rise: 5,340 feet
Rating: Strenuous
Maps: USGS 15' Jay Peak, Irasburg

If you are looking for more rugged trails, steeper mountains, and fewer hikers, then you will enjoy hiking in northern Vermont. This portion of the Long Trail is central to the Green Mountain Club's Long Trail Protection Campaign to preserve these valuable high mountain lands for future generations. In 1985, the Club learned that thiry-four of the sixty-five miles of the Long Trail on private land in northern Vermont were for sale. Convinced that the scenic quality, environment, wildlife habitat, and the continuity of the Long Trail must be saved, the Club started the Long Trail Protection Campaign. As of September 1989, approximately seventeen miles of the Long Trail in central and northern Vermont have been permanently protected.

The first day, you hike to the summit of Belvidere Mountain, where a firetower provides a panoramic view of northern Vermont and the northern summits you traverse. You spend the night at Tillotson Camp, just below the summit of Tillotson Peak.

The second day, you hike 11.7 miles over five summits and through Hazen's Notch. The notch was named after General Moses Hazen, who built a military road in 1778–79 from Peacham to the notch. The hike ends at VT 242 at the base of Jay Peak.

Park one car in the parking area on the south side of VT 242, just west of the height of land, 5.1 miles west of Jay Village, and 6.7 miles east of Montgomery Center.

To reach the trail where your hike begins, drive to, or get dropped off at, the small parking area at the height of land on VT 118, 6.1 miles east of Belvidere Center, and 4.8 miles west of the VT 100 intersection in Eden.

Day One

Total distance: 5.4 miles
Hiking time: 4 hours
Vertical rise: 2,400 feet

Begin your hike on the north side of VT 118, where a trailhead sign indicates a distance of 2.6 miles to Belvidere Saddle and 5.4 miles to Tillotson Camp. Take the white-blazed Long Trail north into the woods and across an abandoned gravel road, the former site of VT 118. Cross Frying Pan Brook and then follow an old logging road. Swing right off the old road and ascend a series of

Tillotson Camp

shelves up the western ridge of the mountain. The trail crests a steep pitch, levels off for a short distance, and climbs again. After 1.75 miles, the trail is rockier and you reach a rock outcrop. Enter a dense boreal forest and continue your climb to Belvidere Saddle at 2.6 miles, where you reach the Forester's Trail junction.

You may want to leave your pack at this junction before climbing to the 3,360-foot summit of Belvidere Mountain. Take a right turn on the narrow, rocky, blue-blazed Forester's Trail to reach the summit. From the summit firetower, which was recently renovated by the Green Mountain Club, you can see the Green Mountains from Camel's Hump in the south to the twin peaks, Big Jay (left) and Jay Peak (right), in the north. Also visible, to their right, are Owl's Head, other Canadian peaks, and Lake Memphremagog. To the east you can see Bald Mountain, Mount Pisgah, Mount Hor, and, to the west, the Cold Hollow Mountains. Look for the asbestos mine on the lower east slope of Belvidere Mountain.

Return to Belvidere Saddle at 3.0 miles and bear left on the Long Trail north, along a white birch and fern-lined ridge. The ridge is often wet and slippery, so be sure to watch your step. Look for occasional views to the east, and a great view almost straight down into the valley below. Continue across several small knobs, with views ahead of Tillotson Peak. After a slight descent, you pass through a wet area and reach Lockwood Pond.

The Green Mountain Club's first major acquisition of land in its Long Trail Protection Campaign was a 1,946 acre tract of land that included Lockwood Pond, as well as the summits of Belvidere Mountain, Haystack Mountain, and Tillotson Peak. This high elevation pond, called an alpine tarn, is the headwaters of the Missisquoi River which flows north into Canada.

Follow the pond's bank, cross the outlet brook, and you soon reach the spur trail to Tillotson Camp at 5.8 miles. The enclosed camp, built in 1939, has bunk space for eight, with campsites nearby.

Day Two

Distance: 11.7 miles
Hiking time: 7 hours
Vertical rise: 2,940 feet

Get an early start, because you will be hiking 11.7 miles over five mountains on your way north to VT 242. Return on the spur trail to the Long Trail and ascend the shoulder of 2,980-foot Tillotson

Peak. An outlook provides a view of Haystack Mountain, which is the next summit you cross. Descend steeply from the ridge, pass a beaver pond, and cross a brook several times as you hike onto a ridge leading to Haystack Mountain. Descend another ridge, then ascend again to reach the blue-blazed spur trail at 8.6 miles that leads to the 3,223-foot summit of Haystack Mountain. Take a short trip to the wooded summit, where you are rewarded with a bird's eye view of Jay and Big Jay peaks. Haystack has outcrops of serpentine, a common mineral, usually oily green and sometimes spotted, which is used for architectural and decorative purposes. The mountain is also the only site of serpentine sandwort in the United States.

Return to the junction and continue along the ridge. You soon begin a very steep descent into Hazen's Notch. Across the notch is the cliff face of Sugarloaf Mountain. The trail levels a little and you cross VT 58 at 10.4 miles. Note the granite marker high on the bank to the right (east) of the trail which commemorates the military road.

Cross VT 58, pass to the left of Sugarloaf Cliff, which looms 700 feet above the road, and descend through an old logging area to Hazen's Notch Camp at 11.0 miles. Take a well-deserved break at the camp, built in 1948 by the Green Mountain Club's Long Trail Patrol.

After your rest, follow the trail behind the camp up the steep shoulder of Sugarloaf Mountain. The trail levels, swings left and right, then drops to a brook and several old logging roads. Climb again to the 2,900-foot summit of Bruce Peak at 13.9 miles. After a short descent, you ascend to the 2,940-foot summit of Buchanan Mountain at 14.4 miles, where there is a good view of Jay Peak. Formerly called Old Splatterfoot, Buchanan

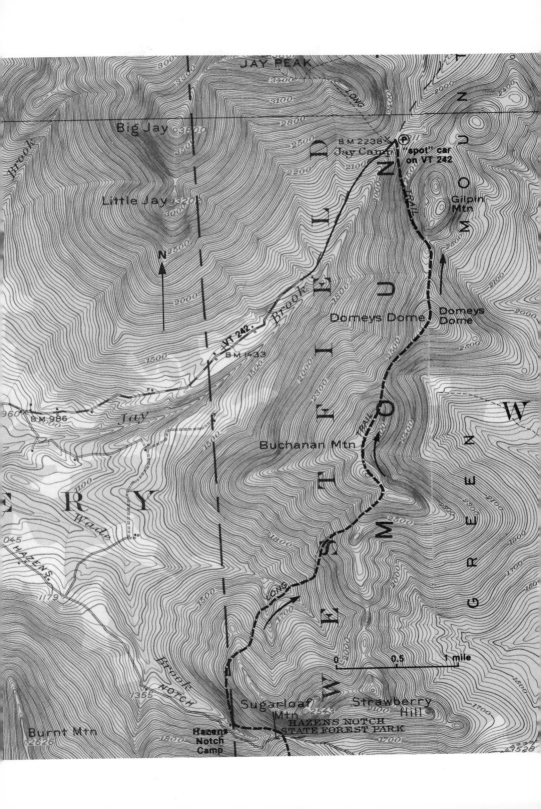

Lockwood Pond on Tillotson Mountain

Mountain was renamed in 1958 in honor of Professor Roy Buchanan of Burlington, who was an active member of the Green Mountain Club for more than thirty years. Just past the summit, you reach Chet's Lookout and a view along the ridge. The lookout was named for Chet Buchanan, Roy's son, who was an active Green Mountain Club member and trail volunteer.

After another short descent, hike on moderate grades to the 2,880-foot sum-mit of Domey's Dome, named after Captain R. H. Domey of St. Albans, who once maintained the trails in this area. Continue over rolling terrain along the side of Gilpin Mountain. Once called Double Top, Gilpin Mountain was renamed, in 1957, after two brothers who were newspaper editors in northern Vermont. Hike downhill on Gilpin's flank, until you reach VT 242 and the parking lot at 17.5 miles.

Monroe Skyline

Total distance: 11.1 miles
Hiking time: 1.5 days, 1 night
Vertical rise: 2,520 feet
Rating: Moderate
Maps: USGS 7.5' Mount Ellen, Lincoln

The Long Trail between Lincoln Gap and the Appalachian Gap (VT 17) is one of the most scenic ridge walks in Vermont. You pass over six mountain summits, three of which are over 4,000 feet in elevation. The Long Trail from Lincoln Gap to the Winooski River is called the Monroe Skyline, after Professor Will S. Monroe, who was instrumental in relocating the trail along this ridgeline.

Your first day is very short (1.8 miles), so you have time to spot cars and arrange equipment. You can also become familiar with carrying a pack, if this is a new or infrequent experience. You can begin on Friday afternoon, as long as you leave ample time (about 2.5 hours, if you haven't hiked in a while) to reach Battell Shelter before dark. Also, since the first day is a short hike, you might consider carrying some extra food/weight for your first evening's meal.

The second day, start early, with a climb up Mount Abraham. Spend the day hiking along the ridgeline, where you enjoy some spectacular views of Vermont, New York's Adirondack Mountains, and New Hampshire's White Mountains. In addition, the ridge is popular with glider pilots, who may sail overhead during your hike. You finish your journey at the Appalachian Gap on VT 17.

Spot a car at the Long Trail parking area on VT 17 at the height-of-land called the Appalachian Gap, which is 6.3 miles west of Irasville and VT 100; 9.6 miles east of the VT 17 and VT 116 intersection; and 12.9 miles east of Bristol.

Begin your hike at the small parking area just east of the height of land in Lincoln Gap. To reach the gap from the eastern side of the mountain, take VT 100 to Lincoln Gap Road (where the sign says, "Lincoln Gap/Bristol") near Warren (0.0), where you turn west. The road turns to dirt at 1.6 miles. At 2.8 miles the road turns back to pavement and ascends to the top of the gap at 4.3 miles.

From the western side of the mountain, drive east of Bristol (0.0) on VT 116/VT 17 to the turnoff to Lincoln and Lincoln Gap at 1.6 miles. Take this turnoff to the town of Lincoln at 5.1 miles. You reach a bridge and United States Forest Service Road 54 at 6.2 miles. At 7.5 miles the road turns to dirt. At 9.3 miles the road turns to pavement again and reaches the top of the gap at 9.9 miles.

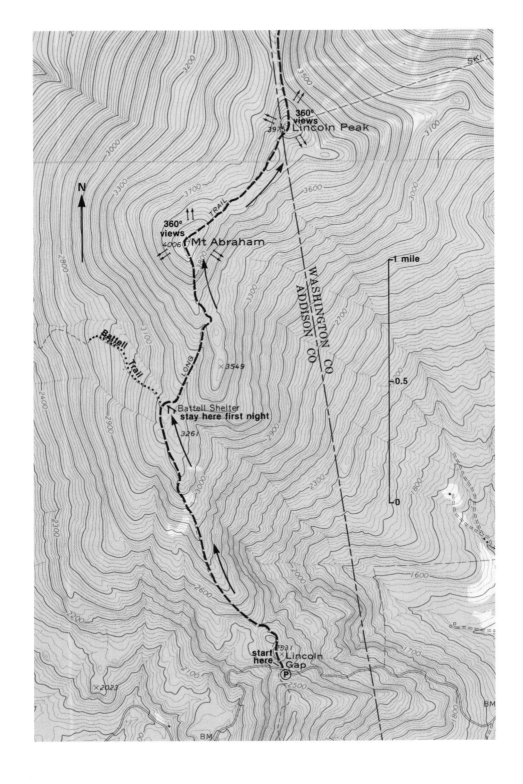

Day One

Total distance: 1.8 miles
Hiking time: 2 hours
Vertical rise: 825 feet

Take the white-blazed Long Trail north from the gap to a Green Mountain National Forest register box. Sign in, then hike up the hillside parallel to the roadway below you. Swing right, climb a small knob, and descend on log steps into a col where the trail switches back along a rock shelf. At 0.4 mile you begin your ascent up the northwestern ridge of Mount Abraham. The trail is quite steep in places, as you ascend a series of plateaus through mixed hard and softwoods.

At 0.8 mile red blazes mark a property line. Climb up an exposed rock ledge scar until you reach a short spur to the left and a good view to the west. Descend into a deep softwood stand and then hike up along a mixed hardwood ridge. A clearing covered with ferns provides a brief break, especially on a sunny day.

At 1.7 miles you pass between two large boulders called "the Carpenters," after two trail workers, and enter another dense softwood stand with a view of Mount Abraham. Now on easier grades, you cross a brook and reach the Battell Trail junction at 1.7 miles.

The trail in this section, quite wide and on easy grades, follows an old carriage road built in the late 1800s by Joseph Battell, proprietor of the Bread Loaf Inn west of Middlebury Gap. In 1901, he cut a trail north to Mount Ellen, possibly the first skyline trail in the Green Mountains.

Turn right at the junction and ascend the Long Trail to Battell Shelter, where you spend the night. The Battell Shelter was constructed in 1967 by campers from Farm and Wilderness Camps using materials airlifted to the site by helicopter. The shelter has bunk space for six to eight hikers and is maintained by the United States Forest Service and the Green Mountain Club. A small spring is located one hundred feet east of the shelter.

Day Two

Total distance: 9.3 miles
Hiking time: 8 hours
Vertical rise: 1,695 feet

If you start very early in the morning, you can climb Mount Abraham in time to see the sun rise over the White Mountains to the east and the valley below covered in a carpet of mist. Just be careful, because the steep, rocky trail is difficult to hike at dawn.

Begin your day's hike uphill on the Long Trail along the old carriage road, with occasional views of the summit ahead. At 0.2 mile you leave the roadway and hike up steep grades, often on exposed bedrock. Look south and enjoy views back down the trail. Next, scramble up an exposed rock face, return briefly to smaller softwoods, and begin your final climb to the summit.

The trees are waist high as you ascend to the open rock summit at 0.8 mile. Three small rock walls provide shelter from the winds as you enjoy one of the best panoramic views in Vermont. To the east, the White Mountains; to the west, the Bristol Cliffs, Lake Champlain, and the Adirondack Mountains; to the south, as far as Killington Peak; and, to the north, as far as Belvidere Mountain. The summit supports a small, rare arctic-alpine plant community, so walk only on the rocks to avoid disturbing any of these endangered plants or the surrounding soils. Beyond the summit, enter the woods and descend until you

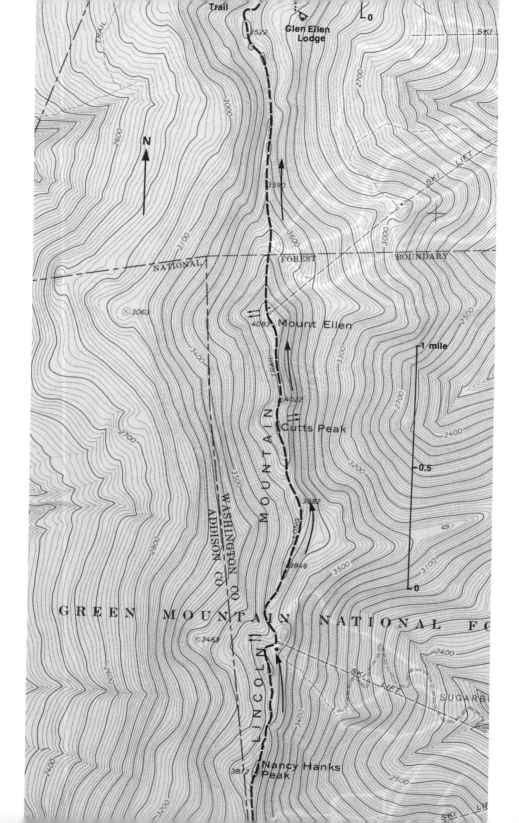

Trail

Glen Ellen
Lodge

3522

SKI

0

N

3063

NATIONAL   FOREST   BOUNDARY

Mount Ellen
4093

1 / mile

Cutts Peak
4022

0.5

3882

3906

WASHINGTON CO
ADDISON CO

MOUNTAIN TRAIL

3846

0

3463

GREEN   MOUNTAIN   NATIONAL   FO

SKI LIFT

SUGARBU

LINCOLN

Nancy Hanks
Peak
3812

SKI LI

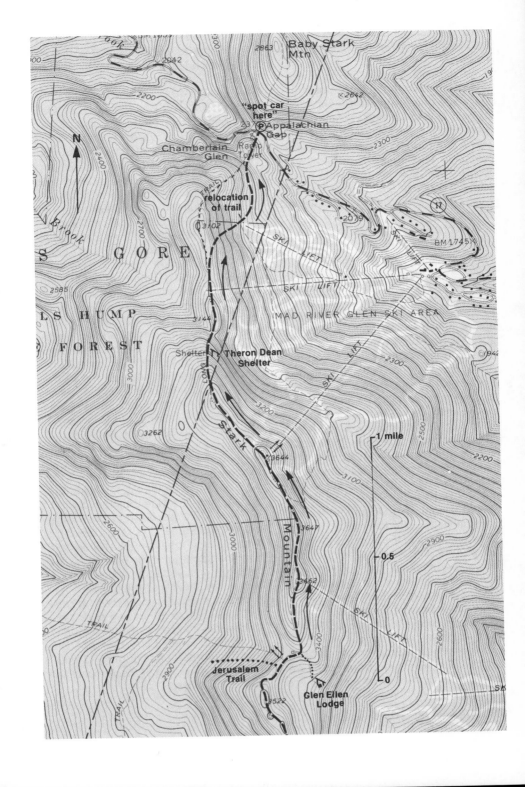

reach the summit of Little Abe and the 3,975-foot summit of Lincoln Peak at 1.6 miles.

As you enter the ski clearing, make a sharp left down to the woods on the west side of the summit. Be very careful of your footing on the exposed rocky west slope, especially since the dramatic views of the Bristol area cause your attention to wander. You return to the woods and follow the now wide and fairly level trail to a lookout of Sugarbush. Allow time to enjoy the view and take a rest.

Continue your hike over the rocky trail on easy grades until you ascend Nancy Hanks Peak (named after a member of a prominent local family) at 2.2 miles and descend to the Castlerock Chair Lift. Bear left and follow the ski trail to Holt Hollow at 3.0 miles where the trail enters the woods. A spring is located 200 feet west of the trail.

Ascend the ridgeline over rolling terrain to the 4,022-foot summit of Cutts Peak at 4.1 miles, where a rock outlook provides another place to rest and enjoy the beautiful view. After descending Cutts Peak, climb to the wooded 4,083-foot summit of Mount Ellen, the third highest mountain in Vermont. Just past the summit is the upper station of the Glen Ellen Chair Lift and good views north of General Stark Mountain, Camel's Hump, and Mount Mansfield. Past the station, the trail makes a sharp left and returns to the woods to avoid the ski trails. Descend the steep western face of the mountain until you reach the Northern Boundary of the Green Mountain National Forest at 4.9 miles.

Here the character of the trail changes abruptly; the forest is denser, there are fewer views, and the ridge is covered with large, moss-covered boulders. At 6.3 miles you reach the Jerusalem Trail junction. Stay on the Long Trail

and ascend a small knob to Orvis Lookout. Continue to the Barton Trail junction, which leads about one quarter of a mile to Glen Ellen Lodge. The lodge was built in 1933 by the Green Mountain Club's Long Trail Patrol. There are excellent eastern views from the lodge of the Mad River Valley, Northfield Mountains, Granite Mountains, and the White Mountains in New Hampshire.

Return to the junction and begin your last major ascent up the west ridge of General Stark Mountain. After reaching the summit, the Long Trail continues along the ridge and follows a ski trail to the top of Mad River Glen's Chair Lift and Stark's Nest at 7.3 miles. Hike uphill past the building, then bear left into the woods. You briefly enter the ski trail before returning to the woods. Scale down over the ridge's exposed rock face, occasionally grabbing roots and lowering yourself over the rock. A ladder is even provided in one particularly difficult spot. After your descent, bear left and follow the moss-covered rock face to Theron Dean Shelter at 8.0 miles. Theron Dean was an active member of the Green Mountain Club during the Club's early years, and was a close friend of Will Monroe.

After resting at the shelter, take a short spur trail on the left to Dean Panorama, your last wide panoramic northern view. Continue down to Dean Cave, a short underground passage which leads back to the main trail 150 feet from the upper junction. Hike along the main trail until you approach a chair lift. Just before the lift, bear left, hike through the woods, and ascend a small rock face. Follow the trail on moderate grades over long switchbacks through a scenic birch forest. Climb over one final knob before descending to VT 17 and the end of your hike at the Appalachian Gap at 9.3 miles.

Little Rock Pond and Clarendon Gorge

Total distance: 14.4 miles
Hiking time: 2 days, 1 night
Vertical rise: 2,775 feet
Rating: Day 1—moderate, Day 2—easy
Maps: GMNF Wallingford SW and NW, USGS 7.5' Rutland

This enjoyable hike along the Long Trail is appropriate for even a novice backpacker. The trail crosses valleys, passes mountain ponds, follows ridgelines, crests mountains, and concludes across a suspension bridge over Clarendon Gorge. There are ample opportunities both days for swimming, as well as numerous scenic vistas.

The suspension bridge over the Gorge was built in 1974. For several years, until the mid-1950s, an old timber bridge spanned the Gorge, but was removed when it decayed and became unsafe. The Green Mountain Club's Killington Section planned a new bridge in 1955 and finally completed construction in the spring of 1957. The bridge held strong until the flood of 1973 washed it away. Four days later, tragedy struck again, when 17-year-old Robert Brugmann attempted to cross the still-swollen river on a fallen tree. He slipped, fell into the stream, and drowned.

A subsequent relocation made such a long detour to reach the bridge in East Clarendon, that the Green Mountain Club started to plan a new bridge. With a design from GMC member Allan St. Peter, major technical assistance from

the Vermont Department of Highways, and memorial gifts from Robert Brugmann's family and friends, construction started in the spring of 1974. The bridge cost almost $8,000; quite a difference from the $700 bridge constructed in 1957! Highway engineers, United States Forest Service personnel, and Green Mountain Club volunteers worked together during various steps along the way to complete the bridge in July 1974.

The first day, you hike past Little Rock Pond and over White Rocks Mountain to Greenwall Shelter, where you spend the night. Little Rock Pond, up to 60 feet deep in places, is one of the most popular day use areas and the highest overnight use area on the Long Trail. The pond, a good fishing spot, is annually stocked with brook trout. Beavers frequent the area, and moose have occasionally been sighted along the pond shore. Careful management is required to preserve the area's natural beauty and fragile shoreline environment. Due to the area's high use, a Green Mountain Club Caretaker is stationed at the site during the hiking season. An overnight use fee is charged.

The second day, you cross VT 140,

hike through overgrown farm lands and pastures, continue along a rocky ridge, and finish across Clarendon Gorge on the suspension bridge.

Spot a car on the south side of VT 103 at the Clarendon Gorge parking area, 2.1 miles east of the US 7 and VT 103 junction, and approximately 5.0 miles south of Rutland. Avoid the temptation to explore the gorge, so that it remains the reward at the end of your journey. Vandalism can be a problem at this parking area; please see the introduction for specific precautions to follow.

To reach the trail where you begin your journey, take US 7 to Danby, where there is a sign pointing east to Mount Tabor and United States Forest Service (USFS) Road-FR 10. Turn east on FR 10 and drive 3.5 miles to the Long Trail Parking Area at Big Black Branch. Because this trailhead is popular with hikers traveling to Little Rock Pond, there is an outhouse, as well as a trailhead information board.

Day One

Total distance: 7.2 miles
Hiking time: 4½ to 5 hours
Vertical rise: 1,275 feet

Begin your hike over easy terrain along the Little Black Branch on an old road. At 0.6 mile you cross the brook on a single I-beam bridge and bear right along the brook. Notice that the brook gets smaller as you cross it again. Continue up the hillside, occasionally on puncheon, small wooden bridges of one or more log or board planks held off the ground on sills. At 1.8 miles you reach a spur trail on the right to Lula Tye Shelter. This shelter was moved from Little Rock Pond to the current location in 1972, by members of the Student Conservation Association, to reduce hiker impact on the pond area. The shelter is named in memory of Lula Tye, who served as Green Mountain Club Corresponding Secretary from 1926 to 1955.

Continue on the Long Trail until you approach the end of Little Rock Pond,

Bridge over Clarendon Gorge

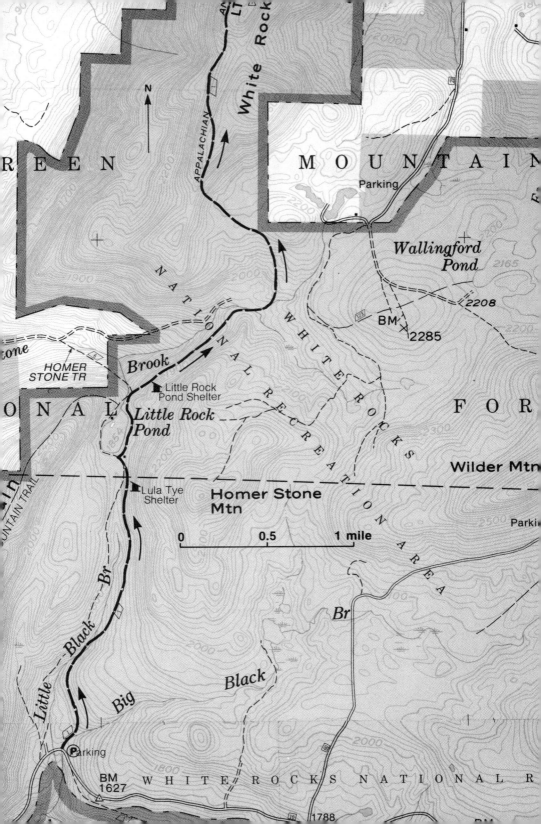

N

GREEN

White Rock

MOUNTAIN

APPALACHIAN

Parking

Wallingford Pond

2165

2208

123

BM
2285

NATIONAL

HOMER
STONE TR

Brook

Little Rock
Pond Shelter

*Little Rock
Pond*

W H I T E   R O C K S

R E C R E A T I O N   A R E A

F O R

Wilder Mtn

Lula Tye
Shelter

Homer Stone
Mtn

Parki

MOUNTAIN TRAIL

0   0.5   1 mile

Br

Br

Little — Black — Br

Big   *Black*

Parking

BM
1627

W H I T E   R O C K S   N A T I O N A L   R

1788

where a signboard explains the pond ecology and area trails. Bear right and come to a tenting area on a knoll behind the Caretaker's tent. A Green Mountain Club Caretaker is stationed at the site during hiking season. Nestled among the mountains at an elevation of 1,854 feet, Little Rock Pond is a scenic place to swim, rest, and cool off. An overnight use fee is charged.

Hike along the shore among dense conifers to the pond outlet at 2.4 miles, where the Green Mountain Trail and, just after, the Homer Stone Brook Trail bear left. Continue straight ahead to a spur trail on the right to Little Rock Pond Shelter. Built by the USFS in 1962, the shelter was moved in 1972 from its former location on the pond's small island.

From the shelter, the Long Trail passes through an old clearing on easy grades, and crosses Homer Stone Brook and the old South Wallingford/Wallingford Pond Road at 3.6 miles. You now begin a sometimes steep and rocky ascent up White Rocks Mountain through dense softwoods and pass just west of the summit at 5.6 miles. An old blue-blazed side trail on the left, which leads to a fantastic view from the top of White Rocks Cliff, may be closed if peregrine falcons are nesting on the cliffs. If the area is posted, please obey the signs.

Descend on the LT to the Keewaydin Trail junction at 6.7 miles. You continue following the Long Trail as you descend to Greenwall Shelter, where you end your day at 7.2 miles. The shelter, a frame lean-to for eight, was built by the USFS in 1962. There are a few tenting sites behind the shelter. A blue-blazed trail leads six hundred feet northeast to a spring, which may fail in very dry weather.

Day Two

Total distance: 7.2 miles
Hiking time: 4½ to 5 hours
Vertical rise: 1,500 feet

Descend from the shelter through an overgrown pasture (be prepared for wet legs), and come to Sugar Hill Road at 0.6 mile. Turn left and follow the road to the junction of FR 19. Cross the road and enter the woods. At 0.9 mile you cross Roaring Brook and reach VT 140. Turn left on VT 140 across a bridge. Turn right on and ascend a gravel road until the trail turns right on an old farm road at 2.4 miles.

After a sharp left turn, you soon return to the woods and begin a steep ascent to the summit of Button Hill at 3.5 miles. The summit is marked by a wooden sign on a tree. Descend from the summit, cross a powerline, and reach a short, unmarked spur trail to the Minerva Hinchey Shelter at 4.6 miles. Minerva Hinchey was the Green Mountain Club Corresponding Secretary for twenty-two years. The shelter is a nice spot to eat lunch and rest before the final leg of your journey.

Continue your hike on the Long Trail up a hardwood ridge and down to Spring Lake Clearing. This meadow is periodically cleared in the spring through prescribed burns by the USFS, Green Mountain Club, and others. By burning at appropriate and safe times, the growth of grasses and ferns is encouraged, while brush and trees are discouraged. This clearing is a National Park Service pilot project to maintain the view and encourage wildlife.

Hike along the ridge, until you reach Airport Lookout, with a good western view of the Otter Creek Valley, Rutland, and the Tacomic Range at 6.2 miles. Descend from the outcrop, cross a

Clarendon Gorge

roadway, and continue down until you reach the Mill River and Clarendon Gorge at 7.1 miles. Cross the gorge on the suspension bridge. As you look down into the deep gorge, picture the river during floods, when the water can rise high enough to touch the bridge! After dropping off your gear at your car, you may wish to further explore and enjoy this scenic area and popular swimming hole.

50

Mount Mansfield

Total distance: 9.3 miles
Hiking time: 2 days, 1 night
Vertical rise: 3,825 feet
Rating: Day 1—difficult, Day 2—moderate
Maps: USGS 7.5' Mansfield

Mount Mansfield, elevation 4,393 feet, is the highest mountain in Vermont and a National Natural Landmark. Because the mountain resembles the profile of a human face when viewed from the east, distinctive points on the ridge are called, south to north, the Forehead, Nose, Upper Lip, Lower Lip, Chin, and Adam's Apple. The Abenakis called the mountain, "Mose-o-de-be Wadso," which means "Mountain-with-the-head-of-a-moose." The mountain probably was named by whites, however, for the town of Mansfield, which was disestablished more than one hundred years ago.

The summit ridge of Mount Mansfield supports a rare and beautiful arctic-alpine plant community. This unique plant-life remains from an era when ice sheets covered northern New England. When the most recent glaciers retreated between eight and twelve thousand years ago, arctic plants grew in exposed areas. As the climate warmed, most of the plants died, except for those on a few mountaintops where the climate resembles the arctic regions a thousand miles to the north of Vermont. Shallow soils, high winds, low temperatures, a short growing season, and high precipitation (one hundred or more inches a year) allow only a few species to survive. Those that remain grow very slowly. The alpine plants absorb five to thirty inches of heavy fog moisture each year in addition to precipitation. Many of the rare plants look like common grass and are difficult to distinguish, so please remember to stay on the trails and rock outcrops.

To learn more about this interesting environment, talk to one of the Ranger-Naturalists stationed on Mount Mansfield during the hiking season. They are there through the cooperation of the University of Vermont, the Mount Mansfield Company, the Vermont Department of Forests, Parks and Recreation, and the Green Mountain Club.

The ridge of Mount Mansfield, owned by the University of Vermont, attracts over 40,000 hikers each year and is included in the Vermont Fragile Areas Registry. While many people prefer direct routes to the top via the toll road and Gondola, there are no fewer than nine approach trails to the summit ridge, over fifteen other trails along the ridgeline, and thirty-one trails in the Mansfield area.

You begin your first day ascending Mount Mansfield from Smuggler's Notch

N

Old Smugglers Face

Smugglers Cave

Bear Pond

Smugglers Notch

Bear Head

Elephants
Head

Spruce Peak

BM ✕ 1803

Lake of the Clouds

Big Spring

Adams Apple

APPROXIMATE BOUNDARY

The Chin

——— 1st day

BM 4393

——— 2nd day

Taft Lodge

Long Trail

MOUNT

MANSFIELD

LONG

Long   Trail

TRAIL

108

STATE

Barnes Camp

Mount Mansfield Hotel

Haselton   Trail

FOREST

BM 3849

Tower

The Nose

Toll

Ski Lift

Road

Ski tow

R

The Forehead

BM ✕ 3120

E

Long Trail

S

APPROX   BDY

APPROXIMATE   BOUNDARY

TOLL   ROAD

0   0.5   1 mile

Bulter
Lodge

to Taft Lodge, a distance of 1.7 miles. Unlike a day hike, a backpacking trip allows you to explore more of the mountain's special points of interest, like Adam's Apple, Lake of the Clouds, and the Chin. In case you decide to leave your backpack somewhere while you explore, bring a day pack with you.

To reach the trailhead, take VT 108 (the Stowe-Jeffersonville Highway) to the Long Trail parking area on the south side of VT 108 just before the picnic area. The ten- to fifteen-car parking lot is 0.7 mile from the Mount Mansfield Ski Area, 8.5 miles north of Stowe, or 9.5 miles south of Jeffersonville.

Day One

Total distance: 3.9 miles
Hiking time: 5 hours
Vertical rise: 2,995 feet

Hike south from the parking area on VT 108 to the Long Trail trailhead, which includes an information board with distances to various points on the mountain. Ascend the steep bank, hike parallel to the highway, and bear right on easier grades through a beech and yellow birch forest. Notice the extensive trail work of steps and waterbars built over the years by the Green Mountain Club to slow the impact of heavy trail use. Waterbars, a drainage system of log or rock construction, are the best defense against trail erosion. A waterbar is composed of three parts: the bar built of log or rock; the apron, a shallow slope to funnel water to the bar and ditch; and the ditch, to carry water off the trail.

Follow along a brook, then zigzag uphill until you reach a registration box. Bear right up a set of stairs, hike over rolling terrain, and cross a small brook twice. Continue your ascent with possible views of Elephant's Head, a great cliff on the east side of the notch.

A series of switchbacks bring you along a ski trail at 1.1 miles, where you can see the Nose and summit towers. Bear right and ascend the sometimes quite steep trail. To your right you can see Spruce Peak Ski Area and Madonna Mountain. Pass a large steel bucket filled with concrete, which was one of several buckets helicoptered to the mountain for ski tower construction. This bucket, obviously, was dropped at the wrong location! Begin a very steep ascent until you reach Taft Lodge at 1.7 miles. This log cabin is the largest and oldest shelter on the Long Trail. Built in 1920, the lodge has bunk space for thirty-two people. A Green Mountain Club Caretaker is in residence during the hiking season and a small fee is charged for overnight use. Due to the area's fragile nature, tent camping is not permitted and there are special policies for waste disposal. Please follow all instructions while at the lodge.

Since Taft Lodge is your day-one destination, you may choose to leave your backpack there and continue your exploration of the mountain with a lighter day pack. If you make the switch, bring along some food, water, a first aid kit, and extra clothes. Remember that weather conditions can change quite rapidly on the summit. Continue up the mountain to a trail junction at Eagle Pass at 2.0 miles. Bear right at the junction on the Adam's Apple Trail, which ascends to the open summit of the Adam's Apple. To the south you see the steep wall of the Chin. Before hiking to the Chin, continue north ascending the Adam's Apple Trail toward Lake of the Clouds, the highest lake in Vermont. At the junction of the Hell Brook and Bear Pond Trails, turn left on the Hell Brook Trail around the Adam's Apple, and return to Eagle Pass at 2.4 miles. At Eagle Pass continue south on the Long Trail and ascend the steep face of the Chin to the summit of Mount Mansfield at 2.7 miles. Remember to stay on the marked trails and rock outcrops to avoid disturbing the fragile alpine vegetation and thin mountain soils. Many of these protected plants look like ordinary grass and are easily damaged by stray footsteps.

From the Chin you have an extensive 360-degree view. To the northeast: the Sterling Range, Laraway Mountain, the Cold Hollow Mountains, Belvidere Mountain, Big Jay, Jay Peak, and the Pinnacle in Canada. To the east: the Worcester Mountains and, beyond them, the Granite Mountains and peaks of the Northeast Kingdom. To the southeast: Mount Washington in New Hampshire and the White Mountains south of the Connecticut Lakes. To the south: the Green Mountains as far south as Killington Peak. To the west: the Adirondack Mountains, including Whiteface Mountain and Mount Marcy. To the northwest you can sometimes see Mount Royal and the skyscrapers in Montreal on a clear day.

After resting and enjoying the spectacular view, continue south along the summit. Hike past the Profanity and Sunset Ridge trails to the junction of the Subway Trail at 3.0 miles on the west side of the ridge. Although fun and exciting, the Subway Trail is extremely difficult and should *not* be attempted with a full backpack or in bad weather. The rocks are extremely slippery when wet. Steeply descend the western face of the mountain through a rock fall area. Agile maneuvering is required around the caves, crevices, and boulders.

After passing through the Subway and ascending a ladder, you quickly return to the ridge on the Subway and Canyon North Extension Trail at 3.3 miles. Back on the ridge, turn left (north) and hike along the Long Trail to the Profanity Trail junction at 3.4 miles. Turn right on the Profanity Trail and steeply descend to Taft Lodge at 3.9 miles.

Day Two

Total distance: 5.4 miles
Hiking time: 3½ to 4 hours
Vertical rise: 830 feet

On the ridge line of Mount Mansfield

View south from Mount Mansfield (Camel's Hump in the distance)

After a good night's rest, return to the summit, at 0.5 mile with your backpack via the Profanity Trail. Hike along the ridgeline past a large rock cairn, called Frenchman's Pile, which marks the site where a hiker was killed by lightning many years ago. If you are caught on the mountain during a thunderstorm, leave the ridge and crouch upon loose rocks that are not immersed in standing water. Do not sit or lie upon the ground, nor touch the soil with your hands because ground currents may travel through your chest. Avoid exposed trees and rock outcrops. Caves and shallow overhangs are dangerous because ground currents jump through these gaps after a strike.

When you reach the top of the Toll Road and the Summit Station at 1.7 miles, leave your pack on the rocks and climb up the Nose for a parting look at the ridge you have just hiked. Return to the Summit Station at 2.1 miles.

The parking lot at the top of the road was the site of the old Mount Mansfield Summit House, which was one of New England's most successful summit hotels until 1958. In 1862, the poet and essayist Ralph Waldo Emerson wrote that, "a man went through the house ringing a large bell and shouting 'Sunrise,'" every morning. Vigorous guests rolled out of bed and climbed the Nose for a prebreakfast sunrise view.

From the summit station, begin your descent down the Toll Road to the Nose Dive Ski Trail, a former ski racecourse, at 2.3 miles. Descend the ski trail and look for a trail sign on the left for the Haselton Trail. This trail, one of the oldest trails on the mountain, is named for Judge Seneca Haselton, the first vice-president of the Green Mountain Club. Continue your descent on the Haselton Trail to the Gondola Base Station at 4.4 miles. Follow the access road down to VT 108, turn left, and hike back to your car at 5.4 miles.

Join the Green Mountain Club

Membership in the Green Mountain Club is open to all who enjoy the outdoors and have a special interest and pride in the mountains of Vermont.

Two types of membership are available:

Section—for those who wish to participate directly in trail maintenance and local events.

At-Large—for those who wish to support the work of the Club, but are not interested in local activities.

All members enjoy the same benefits:
• *The Long Trail News*, which you receive four times a year to keep you informed of Club activities and trail news.
• Discounts on Club publications and special books of regional outdoor interest.
• Reduced fees at most overnight locations served by Club Caretakers.
• Participation in Club-sponsored trips to distant mountains.
• Annual outings, such as the Annual Meeting, with recreational hikes, cycling trips, a special dinner, and entertainment; and the Intersectional, a week of fun-filled activities at a camp in Vermont.

As a member of the Green Mountain Club, you will contribute to the maintenance and preservation of the entire Long Trail system, as well as efforts to preserve the environmental quality and beauty of Vermont's mountains.

Section Membership

GMC Sections are semi-autonomous local "chapters" which conduct hikes and other activities, and maintain a portion of the Long Trail System. They are as follow:

Bennington VT
Brattleboro VT
Bread Loaf—Middlebury, VT
Burlington VT
Connecticut CT
Killington—Rutland, VT
Laraway—Northern VT
Manchester VT
Montpelier VT
*New York—NY, NJ
Ottauquechee—Woodstock, VT
Pioneer Valley—Western MA
Sterling—Morrisville, VT
Worcester—Eastern MA

Dues schedule is for provisional New York Section membership.

MEMBERSHIP AND ORDER FORM

Name(s) _____

Address (street and mailing address, if different) _____

_____

_____

Telephone Number_____

Please circle one membership category:

Individual* 22.00
Family (includes children under 18)* ...30.00
Sponsor (Individual or Family) 45.00
Defender (Individual or Family) 70.00
Protector (Individual or Family) 100.00
Non-profit or Youth Group 30.00

Business or Corporation 100.00
Life Membership.................................500.00
Dual Life Membership (Two Adults)...750.00

*Students (full time) and Seniors (70 and over) may take a discount of $7.00

Quantity	Title	Member · Non-Member Prices	Total
_____	*Guide Book of the Long Trail*	7.95 · 9.95	____
_____	*Day Hiker's Guide to Vermont*	7.95 · 9.95	____
_____	*End to End*	6.35 · 7.95	____
_____	Trail Map: Camel's Hump	2.35 · 2.95	____
_____	Trail Map: Mt. Mansfield	3.15 · 3.95	____
_____	*Tundra Trail Guide*	.80 · 1.00	____
_____	*Green Mountain Adventure* — Softcover	7.95 · 9.95	____
_____	Long Trail Cloth Patch for sleeve or pack	2.50 · 3.25	____
_____	Long Trail Decal	.50 · 1.25	____
_____	GMC Cloth Patch for sleeve or pack	2.50 · 3.25	____
_____	GMC Decal	.50 · .75	____
_____	"The Long Trail: A Footpath in the Wilderness"	Free · Free	____
_____	"Day Hiker's Vermont Sampler"	Free · Free	____
_____	"Winter Trail Use in the Green Mountains"	Free · Free	____

Postage & Handling

Order under $4.99 ....$.75
Order $5.00 to $20.00 ....$2.00
Order $20.01 to $40.00 ....$2.75
Order $40.01 and over $3.75
First Class ....add $.50 per book
International orders ....add $2.00

- Sorry, no charge cards accepted
- Prices subject to change without notice.
- U.S. Funds only, please.
- If only free publications are ordered, please enclose a self-addressed, stamped legal size envelope.

Order total	
5% sales tax (VT res.)	
Postage	
Subtotal	
Membership Dues	
Deductible Contribution	
Total Amount Enclosed	

Also from The Countryman Press
and Backcountry Publications

The Countryman Press and Backcountry Publications, long known for fine books on travel and outdoor recreation, offer a range of practical and readable manuals.

Hiking Series:

50 Hikes in the Adirondacks, $11.95
50 Hikes in Central New York, $11.95
50 Hikes in Central Pennsylvania, $10.95
50 Hikes in Connecticut, $11.95
50 Hikes in Eastern Pennsylvania, $10.95
50 Hikes in the Hudson Valley, $10.95
50 Hikes in Lower Michigan, $12.95
50 Hikes in Massachusetts, $11.95
50 More Hikes in New Hampshire, $12.95
50 Hikes in New Jersey, $11.95
50 Hikes in Northern Maine, $10.95
50 Hikes in Ohio, $12.95
50 Hikes in Southern Maine, $10.95
50 Hikes in West Virginia, $9.95
50 Hikes in Western New York, $12.95
50 Hikes in Western Pennsylvania, $11.95
50 Hikes in the White Mountains, $12.95

Other Books on Northern New England

New Hampshire: An Explorer's Guide, $16.95
Maine: An Explorer's Guide, $16.95
Vermont: An Explorer's Guide, $16.95
Waterfalls of the White Mountains, $14.95
New England's Special Places, $12.95
Family Resorts of the Northeast, $12.95
Walks and Rambles in the Upper Connecticut River Valley, $14.95
Canoe Camping Vermont & New Hampshire Rivers, $7.95
30 Bicycle Tours in New Hampshire, $10,95
25 Bicycle Tours in Maine, $9.95
25 Bicycle Tours in Vermont, $8.95
25 Mountain Bike Tours in Vermont, $9.95
25 Ski Tours in Vermont, $8.95
25 Ski Tours in New Hampshire, $8.95

We offer many more books on hiking, walking, fishing and canoeing in New York State, New England, the Midwest, and the Mid-Atlantic states—plus books on travel, nature, and many other subjects.

Our titles are available in bookshops and in many sporting goods stores, or they may be ordered directly from the publisher. When ordering by mail, please add $2.50 per order for shipping and handling. To order or obtain a complete catalog, write The Countryman Press, Inc., P.O. Box 175, Woodstock, Vermont 05091.